FLYING BLIND

Geoffrey Morley-Mower in the first photograph
after the presentation of wings, 1937.

FLYING BLIND

A MEMOIR OF BIPLANE OPERATIONS OVER WAZIRISTAN IN THE LAST DAYS OF BRITISH RULE IN INDIA

by
Wing Commander Geoffrey Morley-Mower,
DFC, AFC

Yucca Tree Press

First Printing   June 2000

Morley-Mower, Geoffrey

   FLYING BLIND: A Memoir of Biplane Operations Over Waziristan in the Last Days of British Rule in India.
          1. World War II, 1939-1945 - British Air Force.   2. World War II, 1939-1945 - British India.   3. Biplane operations.
          I. Geoffrey Morley-Mower.   II. Title.

Library of Congress Catalog Card Number: 99-69920

ISBN: 1-881325-40-7

AUTHOR'S NOTE

This book is about the joy of flying—the intoxicating and dangerous freedom to move through the blue air in three directions at once. It is also a history, tied to my flying log book and my personal journal. The period is 1937-1941. World War II had broken out in Europe in September 1939, but I was stationed in India where time stood still. The overseas British continued to live in splendour, waited upon by armies of servants, as if nothing had happened. I found myself flying biplanes of ancient vintage over the most exotic frontier in the world, keeping order among tribes that had not changed since the invasion of India by Mahmud of Ghazni in the Middle Ages. It is also a history of army and air operations in tribal Waziristan during the last years before the idea of controlling them was abandoned forever. The British Empire has since passed away and all the old-fashioned aircraft are in museums.

The commando tactics of the Wazirs and their legendary cruelty has been dealt with before (*eg*, *Bugles and a Tiger* by John Masters) but never adequately from the point of view of an airman in an open cockpit, out of touch with the troops he serves except by picking up messages from the ground with a manually lowered hook! Because I was located at Miramshah, a mud and brick fort close to the Afghan frontier, I was privy to the politics of the region and the curious attitude of the British officials who seemed to sympathize more with the lawless tribes than the Indian Army which was seeking to maintain order in the province.

I joined the Royal Air Force with defective eyesight, and had some lucky escapes while training, but finally had to appeal to King George VI in order to retain my flying status. I believe this is a unique example of youthful cockiness; and although the privilege of an officer to appeal to the monarch is well known I have no knowledge of anyone else doing it, much less getting away with it!

When the book ends I am on a Sunderland flying boat touching down on the River Nile a mile or so from the great pyramid. General Irwin Rommel is threatening the security of Britain's base in the Middle East and I am about to join an Australian fighter reconnaissance squadron in support of the Eighth Army. That story, which defined my youth, is told in *Messerschmitt Roulette* (Phalanx, 1993).

ACKNOWLEDGEMENTS

My first acknowledgement is to Kimberley John Lindsay of Hemmingen, Germany, who has been the first reader and editor of this manuscript and to whom I owe much good advice and encouragement. His father and grandfather were both officers in the Australian army and both earned the Military Cross for bravery in action. He wrote to me in appreciation of my book, *Messerschmitt Roulette*, and we at once achieved a rapport which led to this collaboration. He is a collector of medals and an expert on military history, with a special interest in British India. It has been a delight to be in his safe, critical hands throughout the writing of this book.

I am grateful to my family and friends for their love and support in this enterprise; to my sons, Anthony and Stephen and to my daughter, Bernadette. To Wing Commander George Topliss and Eda Topliss for their help in finding photographs and for their kind hospitality on my research visits to England. To Diana Barthold for photographs and generous help, and to Sheila Miller for photographs of her first husband, Michael Savage. To my brother Peter for much hospitality and for details of his long and arduous war career. To Patrick Biggie for details of his career in the Foreign Service and for his comments on the manuscript. To Mrs P.C. Lal of New Delhi, India, for the provision of her husband's memoirs, countless letters and much indispensable assistance in the identification of people in old photographs. In a special way I need to acknowledge the help of writer Christopher Isherwood, with whom I spent one afternnon at his home overlooking the Pacific in Los Angeles. His indispensable advice was to write and rewrite and rewrite, and never to be abashed by the awfulness of first drafts.

William J. Miller, the author of *Mapping for Stonewall,* gave me indispensable advice on the tricky question of what to put in and what to leave out. I would like to thank him for his expertise and his understanding of my difficulties.

Dr Elizabeth Stein, my colleague in the English Department of James Madison University, deserves special mention. A creative writing teacher, she not only read both of my books but drew attention to their deficiences. This kind of help is superior to vacuous praise and much harder to deliver. I cannot thank her enough for making me expand my narrative where the scene had been sketched but not painted in.

Lastly I wish to thank my beloved wife, Mary, for her encouragement of my desire to write these books and her willingness to give me the time to do so. Without her co-operation there is no way they could have been begun, much less completed. In addition, she provided a good deal of the material on the family life of British people in India. To sum up, she is the "only begetter" of these ensuing pages.

CONTENTS

LIST OF ILLUSTRATIONS

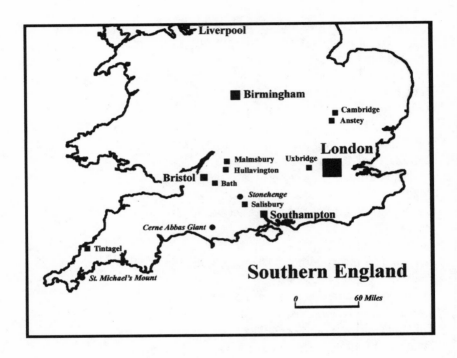

Liverpool

■ Birmingham

■ Cambridge
■ Anstey

■ Malmsbury   Uxbridge
■ Hullavington   ■   London ■

Bristol ■
     ■ Bath
          ● Stonehenge
          ■ Salisbury
Cerne Abbas Giant ●   ■ Southampton

■ Tintagel

St. Michael's Mount

Southern England

0   60 Miles

Courtesy: Terrence Haney

1

Flying Blind
3rd September 1937 to 28th April 1938

Dr John Gubbins, our family physician, was a large, good-looking Irishman who had one leg shorter than the other. When a member of the family was ill we would watch him as he arrived in our driveway in his sports car. The rear seat had been removed and the driver's seat had been re-positioned to give room for his longer leg, which was inflexible. He would struggle out of his car and lurch up to our front door, swinging his leather doctor's bag to balance himself. I knew he would help me if he could and I decided to go to his surgery and consult him. I had a notion that there was a drug he could prescribe that would make me see a little better for a long enough period of time to pass an eye test. It was the first time I had been to his surgery, a rather gloomy house in West Ealing, the suburb of London where we lived.

"If you've poor eyesight," he said, smiling at me, "what makes you think you could fly an aeroplane anyway?"

"Oh, I'm sure I can fly," I replied. "I just have to pass that damned examination."

He was amused by me. He didn't think I had a ghost of a chance of deceiving the RAF doctors, but he got into the spirit of the thing.

"Well," he said, leaning back in his swivel chair, "there are a number of drugs that can improve the vision temporarily, but they are all toxic and they'll increase your heart beat and put up your blood pressure, even in small quantities. Do you realize that?"

He talked on, thinking aloud, going through a list of drugs that one normally associates with murder trials.

"I think I can give you something. It's just a small amount. It won't kill you." I think he mentioned strychnine, but it might have been an equally deadly poison.

"Take it about fifteen minutes before your eye test. And don't take it if you are just about to have your interior examined or they might think you are on your last legs."

He laughed heartily. When he was enjoying himself, his manner and phrasing became more Irish .

"Once they've looked at your heart and blood pressure, take it and be damned."

I had received a non-committal reply to my application for a commission and was directed to report to the Air Ministry, Kingsway, for my medical board. The waiting room was crowded with hopefuls like myself. They all seemed to be wearing the same Harris tweed sports coats, grey flannels and green porkpie hats. Each specialist had his own room and our names were called by a corporal who added the room number in a loud military voice. Clearly there was no special sequence to the examinations. By good luck my first interview was for heart and blood pressure. As soon as I was out of the doctor's office, I went to the lavatory and took the powder. Within ten minutes I was sent in for the dreaded eye test. It was extraordinarily perfunctory. I was simply lined up in front of a board with rows of letters, decreasing in size from top to bottom.

"Stand behind this line," said the doctor. He was wearing a white coat, unbuttoned, over his blue RAF uniform.

"Put your hand over your left eye and read off the lowest line you can see clearly."

He looked down at the papers on his desk and began writing. It was so easy to cheat. I could use both eyes by simply opening my fingers slightly. Possibly Dr Gubbin's magic powder had given me gimlet vision. I read off the bottom line proudly.

That's how it all started. I had been wearing glasses since the age of twelve. My desk was at the back of the class and I was often unable to make out what was written on the blackboard. One of the masters at my school in London discovered this and sent a note to my parents. It turned out that I had an astigmatism which reduced my visual acuity from 6/6, which represented perfect eyesight in the RAF code, to 6/12, which was unacceptable. I saw Mr Buck, the oculist who had a shop near the tube station at Ealing Broadway. He also told me I had no chance of passing the RAF tests. I didn't believe him.

My motives for joining up in 1937 (an ominous date in history) were not to defend my country or to fight a war. Our generation had grown up in the aftermath of the 'War to End War' and it was an article of faith that the mistake would never be repeated. As a child I was familiar with the limbless ex-servicemen sitting on the cold pavements with their tin cups set out to collect pennies, and their crude placards detailing their griefs. You could not have convinced me that the German lads I'd met on European holidays would ever be a threat to peace. The pilots in our entry who wanted to fly bombers believed they were getting free training for the commercial air lines. The fighter boys were in it for glamour and prestige. I just wanted to get airborne and see the world.

Before we were commissioned and allowed to wear uniform, we had to report to Air Service Training, Anstey, an airfield in the

Airfield at Anstey, 1937.

flat country near Cambridge. There we were given our first flying experience on Avro Cadets and Miles Magisters. The Magisters were monoplanes, the Cadets biplanes, and, both were painted yellow to indicate they were training aircraft. The instructor sat in the front cockpit and the student behind. It was a weeding out process and about half the entry of thirty would-be-pilots were returned to civilian.life.

I ran into trouble at once with my flying instructor, Flight Lieutenant 'Drip' Williams. He was a retired officer, teaching flying in this commercial enterprise that tested pilots for the RAF. He was nicknamed Drip because in the damp, cold air of England his beaky nose rarely failed to suspend a globule of moisture. I didn't have much difficulty with landings, steep turns or recovery from spins. My problem was in seeing the windsock. From the circuit height of 1000 feet all I could see was a white blur.

There were no runways at Anstey. The airfield was just a large grass square, and behaviour on the circuit depended on seeing the windsock. There was a landing 'T,' which indicated the official direction of landing and take off, but I could not see that either. Naturally I did everything to disguise my disability. I would bumble around the airfield waiting for him to lose his temper with me. Eventually he would come out with a testy remark. "Morley, you're always late turning downwind." Thank you, Drip. Now I know which way the windsock is pointing!

He knew there was something wrong with me, but he couldn't diagnose it. Many times I functioned perfectly. When another Magister was approaching to land, I could simply follow it in. He would praise me on these occasions, hoping to improve my consistency by encouragement. It didn't work. Inexplicable bungling would occur just as he was preparing to send me solo. He delayed giving me that honour until I was the last remaining 'live' candidate.

I confided in one of the other students, a handsome fellow who was a little older than the rest of us. It's strange that I remember his initials. C.C.F. Cooper. He had been to America to study chiropractics, in the hope of setting himself up as a spine manipulator in Britain, but he had run out of cash and joined the air force. He was one of those super competent guys. Some Yankee know-how had rubbed off on him.

"You'll get scrubbed if they find out," he said. He had a low brow and a nice worried frown. "I can just see Sadie Veal's face." 'Sadie' C.D. Veal, was the chief Flying Instructor, a precise little man who always gave the final tests himself, passing the fortunate and delivering the coup de grace to the crestfallen failures. I could see him pursing his lips at my chicanery. But I hadn't entirely given up hope.

"If Drip Williams will put me up for my first solo," I said, "I've got a chance. I'm getting the hang of the circuit. The wind doesn't change around that much. If other planes are flying it'll be a piece of cake."

"I wouldn't want to fly if I was half blind," Cooper said.

"I'm not really blind, Cliff. Just a bit fuzzy round the edges. With my glasses on I'm a hundred percent."

"It sounds dicey to me. I'd stick to bicycles if I were you."

December 17th, 1937, was Doomsday. The weather was perfect for flying, crisp and cold, bright sunshine, no cloud. My prospects for entering the Royal Air Force as a pilot, however, were dim and dark. I had already flown seven hours and twenty five minutes of dual instruction, and it was generally believed among the students that five hours was average and seven hours the limit. If one hadn't gone solo before seven hours it was kaput! I knew I was being put up for suspension.

The procedure was scrupulously fair and judicial. Two instructors had to agree on the unworthiness of a student, and Sadie Veal authorized their verdict. When I arrived at the hangar after breakfast that morning Drip Williams was already kitted out like an Arctic explorer, with fur lined boots, inner and outer flying suits and a brown wool scarf that looked as if it had been knitted by his wife. He was standing in front of a lectern which held the Flight Authorization book and was signing lucky soloists off on their flights. He called me over.

"Morley," he said, looking at me coldly. "Mr Tribe is going to fly with you.

Pilot Officer Tribe was a big thickset man with thinning red hair. An ex-sergeant pilot who had been commissioned after twenty years of active flying, he was known to be the most qualified instructor on the staff, having taught at the Central Flying School, Upavon. His job that day was simply to check out that I was no good.

As I taxied out in my Magister behind three other aircraft the scene was unique. It was the climactic moment of the weeding out process at Anstey. Everyone was going solo except me. The instructors had gathered on the tarmac to watch their students perform circuits and landings. Every minute some aircraft touched down on the broad acreage of grass. Eight aircraft were flying the rectangular circuit of the airfield at a thousand feet above the ground, waiting for a chance to turn into wind for a landing. Any fool with half my eyesight could tell the wind direction without benefit of windsock or landing T. I felt a surge of confidence, a sort of mystical certainty that my luck was going to hold.

My first and second landings were so satisfactory that Tribe, who'd been maintaining a monastic silence in the front seat, began to chat amiably to me. He knew I was O.K and he was going to enjoy telling Drip Williams that he'd been all wrong about me!

"Very nice landings," he shouted. "But try to judge your approach so you don't land halfway into the field. Let me have her a moment."

He turned smoothly crosswind and cut the engine.

"There. Now you take over and land as close to the boundary as you can."

A minute or so later I whistled over the fence and came to a stop near to the aircraft line up.

"Well done," he said. "Keep your engine running." He ran across to where Williams was standing and I saw them talking animatedly. Eventually Williams walked over, his helmet dangling from his left glove.

"Switch off the engine and come in. You'll have your CFI test after lunch."

I ate a hearty meal and prayed for a crowded circuit. And so it turned out. Veal was very distant and formal. He didn't want to get emotionally involved with a young fellow whose life ambition he might have to destroy. He barely spoke to me. Just the necessary words.

"Are you strapped in?"

"Yes, sir."

"Taxi to the edge of the field and take off in your turn. Keep a good look out for other aircraft landing. We're rather busy today."

Busy was no exaggeration. The air was buzzing with activity. Strings of tiny yellow planes were following each other into land. Eager soloists were bouncing and going round again. I produced three good landings and Veal made no comment. I don't think he spoke to me, except to tell me to try another take off and landing. When we came in, he sent me solo. I saw him speaking earnestly to Williams as I walked out triumphantly to my plane.

I was through! I could walk on water. The hell with C.C.F. Cooper and his pedal bikes! I was going to cleave the bright air with the rest.of them, unchaperoned by Drip Williams or anyone else. I put my gloved hand on the frail fabric of the wing and said to myself, "I *am* going to be a pilot, dammit! I *am* going to be a pilot!"

As soon as I'd taxied out from the line of Magisters and Cadets I fished out a pair of spectacles from the pocket of my flying suit. I parked crosswind and settled them on my nose. What a relief to see sharp outlines, the steady windsock, blades of grass, aircraft letters, a man sitting behind the plate glass of the control tower, even the recognizable faces of other pilots in their machines.

I took off and saw the earth from the air. It was like an etching. I saw the wire fence surrounding the field, the bright yellow butterflies that now were parked Magisters, woods sharp and clear as in a toyshop, farmhouses and outbuildings neat as a pin, the black and white cattle in the meadows arranged by hand. Without Williams in the front seat I could let my eyes wander. I noticed the weather vanes that were never there before, and could read the time from the church clock. I followed a baker's van down a narrow lane and read his name off the side. In a medium turn I was steady as a magic carpet.

After an intoxicating twenty minutes I flew back to Anstey and landed three times as instructed. When I taxied in, my glasses safely in my overall pockets, Williams was on the tarmac with his parachute and helmet. He yelled at me not to shut down the engine.

"Well done," he said grimly, as soon as he'd settled himself in the cockpit and connected the speaking tube. "We're going to practice some more steep turns and spins for half an hour. Where did you get to? I told you three landings only." In my excitement I had forgotten that he would be watching me.

"I was flying around, getting the hang of it before I came in," I replied.

Grunt!

It is possible that Williams was miffed at the way his rejection test had turned out. Perhaps his judgement had been challenged by Veal. Anyhow, I was assigned to a new instructor, who turned out to be Tribe. It is possible that he asked for me. I like to think so. He flew exclusively on Cadets, so I flew these biplanes for the remainder of the course, clocking up sixty-five hours on type.

I loved the Cadets and despised Magisters, which were-up-to-date flying machines with disgusting innovations like wing flaps, unknown to my heroes, Captain Albert Ball and Baron Manfred von Richthofen. The standard monoplane approach is to motor in against the drag of the flaps. There is some skill involved in this, but no elegance. The classic biplane approach is a pure glide with shut off engines, the pilot relying on his judgement of height and windspeed to land on a given spot on the grass. It was considered to be a fault of style to use the engine to save a badly judged glide, and many an aviator has slapped into the boundary fence in his reluctance to use the power of his engine. If you drop the wing of a biplane and hold the nose up with opposite rudder, it will slip in a controlled manner towards the earth. If you try to perform the same maneuver in a monoplane, the large keel surface resists slippage and nothing beautiful or controlled will result. Sergeant Tribe, a big red-faced sandy haired man, enjoyed showing off his advanced biplane skills to an enthusiastic youngster, and I egged him on with my heartfelt praises.

Diary entry: 13th January 1938

Sergeant Tribe is a terrific pilot and he shows this close to the ground. He's the only "A I" category flying instructor in A.S.T. and the only ex-NCO as well. He may be rubbing it in to the officer class that he's the most qualified person around here, Coming in to land he sideslips with very positive movements, timed to be of equal duration, like an aerial dance. The second sideslip takes him over the boundary fence and down to ground level, his wing almost brushing the grass before straightening out for a touchdown. At this point he'll swishtail, kicking off excess speed. In the back cockpit I can follow the ample movements of the rudder and stick, smooth and confident, inches from

the surface. When he touches down with a whisper from
the wheels, I shout my approval through the Gosport
tubes. Which I think he likes.

'Gosport' tubes were the only method of communication
between the cockpits, and shouting was necessary because there
was no other artificial aid to hearing. It was like shouting down a
deaf person's ear trumpet, when the trumpet itself is being
swamped with the sound of slipstream and engine noise. It
reminded me somewhat of the primitive speaking tubes for calling servants which existed in every room of my parents' Victorian
house, and with which the children were not permitted to play.

Sergeant Tribe would also perform superb aerobatics; but I
wasn't impressed by his loops and barrel rolls, which held no danger of sudden death if not skilfully done. What I admired was the
discipline and cadence of his sideslips, the way his cocked wing
would flirt with the ground, and the rumble of his landings—
impossible to convey to non-pilots—as the feathery light frame
stalls in exact concert with the first touch of rubber on grass. It
was with Sergeant Tribe that I fell in love with the art of flying,
knowing I was too green to practice it, but filled with ambition to
fly well.

When the initial course was over we were commissioned (a
document which I have now lost, signed by King George VI,
arrived in the mail), designated Pilot Officers on Probation, and
reassembled at the Royal Air Force Depot, Uxbridge, to be fitted
for our uniforms. Uxbridge is on the western outskirts of London,
a dull suburb but convenient for its purpose as a training centre
for airmen. The Depot stood on the main road, crowded with
shops, double decker buses and motor traffic, surrounded by a
high grey wall like a prison. Inside the gates were grandiose
administrative buildings, ugly barracks, playing fields and square
concrete parade grounds. Squads of airmen in fatigues kept the

"The Greatcoat," with the collar illegally turned up
to look like a Balkan Count!

place neurotically tidy, and every post was painted white. There was no peace and quiet at Uxbridge. All day one could hear the raucous shouting of drill sergeants, the thud of boots to the ground and the roar of traffic beyond the wall. It was a sad contrast to the rural paradise of Anstey.

There was no ready made or off-the-peg tailoring in those days. The military tailors from London sent their representatives to woo us and we met them in one of the reception rooms of the gloomy officers mess. I yielded to a Dickensian, wheedling, hand-wringing tailor from Plumbs in Victoria Street, who afterwards fitted me in the back of his shop, draping me with cut-out portions of cloth, talking all the time in a sweet cockney voice, his mouth full of pins. Most of the pilots went to Gieves, the more fashionable tailor.

Diary entry: 28th February 1938

It's a pity our uniforms take so long to make, because this place is a purgatory. Yesterday we had a lecture on the history of the Royal Air Force which would have sent anyone to sleep. Nothing about flying at all, just junk about command structures. Today a fat old doctor showed some disgusting slides of people with their genitals dropping off, and he went on at wearisome length on the primary, secondary and tertiary stages of syphilis. He talked as if we were going to run off to Piccadilly and acquire a disease as soon as the lecture was over. Very strange! For an hour every morning we're drilled on the square by a different NCO who shouts obscenities at us, while hypocritically calling us "gentlemen." We look a pitiful sight in our grey flannel trousers and porkpie hats and suede shoes, our faces scarlet from the open cockpits. If no one knew we were pilots, they'd think we were terminal drunks.

The RAF airfield, Hullavington, 1938.

Once outfitted we were finished with Uxbridge. Ever since Oliver Cromwell's time the English people have had a horror of standing armies, and in 1938 we were forbidden to wear our uniforms in public. We turned up at No. 9 Flying Training School, Hullavington, in civilian clothes, toting our heavy suitcases, stuffed with two uniforms, a mess kit for evening, and two military hats. I never liked to wear a round hat with a peak, because having a round face it looked as if one pudding were balanced on another. My choice was the 'fore-and-aft,' which you could perch on the side of your skull and which reminded me of old photographs of flying aces in the War to End War. Surprisingly, we were allowed to use whatever hat we liked best, except for parades when the round hat was worn.

Hullavington in Wiltshire was set in the most beautiful landscape in the world to fly over. It rolled gently and varied between meadow and plough, woodland and downland. Forgotten hamlets were connected by a maze of narrow high-hedged lanes, cows everywhere and sheep scattered like pearls. There were thatched villages with roses climbing over the cottage walls, and great houses of Palladian magnificence, like Badminton, just off the airfield circuit. The city of Bath nestled in a ring of hills, its crescent of eighteenth century houses overlooked by a medieval cathedral. Every time we rose into the air we viewed this civilized wilderness. Cotswold villages, like Castle Combe, were within biking distance. None of us had cars, so there was a rush to hire bicycles in Cirencester, a small town which was once a Roman fort, and the centre of government for the west of England. The ruins of Malmesbury Abbey stood on a hill overlooking the local scene.

A useful landmark to me, with my imperfect eyesight, was the Roman road called the Fosse Way. It ran straight as a die from Lincoln in the east midlands to Axminster in the southwest; and it passed right through Cirencester. It stood out from the air because nothing in the English countryside is straight except the old Roman roads. The centuries had buried the Fosse Way beneath the fields and farms, but from the air its path could be clearly seen. It would follow a local road for a few miles and then the modern highway would wander off, but the Fosse Way would continue on as a distinct trace on the landscape. The majority of pilots could see Hullavington at a distance as they approached it; the big hangars, the impressive permanent buildings, the square grass airfield, the dark shape of Malmesbury. But I could not be sure of any of these things. They were blurs which I could only identify close up. What the lucky majority did not see—and what I saw as the main characteristic of the scene—was the dead straight line that passed through the centre of Cirencester and brushed Hullavington as it made its way towards Bath, and which told me that I was on track to base.

My instructor was Flight Sergeant Boyd, a tight-lipped Irishman from Dublin. In the manner of those days he called me "Sir" and I addressed him as "Flight Sergeant," in spite of the fact that my fate lay in his.hands. It wasn't long before he discovered that there was something wrong with me, though he diagnosed it incorrectly. The words that he enunciated in his precise brogue were "inattention" and "carelessness." I was a good student and could learn to fly well, he would explain, but must guard against losing concentration. "Flying demands the most absolute concentration," he would say. "Not until you switch off your engine, and hand the aircraft over to your ground crew, can you afford to relax."

On a day when the wind was light and variable I met disaster. Boyd had been showing me forced landings—that is, the procedure and technique for getting your machine on the ground in one piece after an engine failure. The forced landing field was a patch of unmarked grass beside a crescent of woods. It was an idyllic spot in a setting of extraordinary natural beauty, but I gave my whole attention to the problem Boyd had given me.

"Your engine has failed," he said, pulling back the throttle against the stop. "Now look around for a suitable landing place."

My vision was equal to such emergencies. I could see a patch of well-mowed turf with the best of them. Boyd was pleased with the way I maneuvered downwind, detouring to keep the field in sight as height was lost, and then turning into wind, overshooting as taught, and sliding to the ground in one careful, unadventurous sideslip to the boundary of the field. However, when we arrived back at Hullavington, the people in the control tower had perceived a change in wind direction and had turned the landing T 180 degrees to the previous landing path. If there had been other planes around I would have seen what had happened, but the circuit was clear. I made a good landing and Boyd allowed me to complete it, to ensure my maximum humiliation. Then he opened up the throttle and gave me as close as he could get to an angry lecture. "You landed downwind!" he roared, his voice expressing outrage and disgust.

On the ground he was once again quiet and serious, speaking about the certainty of violent death for the pilot who will not concentrate on every detail of the pilot's craft. I had failed to check the signals square. A mortal sin.

What could I say? He could not have imagined my real dilemma.

Such a mistake never occurred again or my career would have ended then and there. As the course progressed more of my flying was solo, when my glasses could be used. A mark of all this trouble and deception did, however, remain. An assessment was placed in my log book which, in the nature of such things, stands forever. My final grade as a pilot, signed by the Chief Flying Instructor of No. 9 Flying Training School, reads; AVERAGE; and underneath in his handwriting is scrawled the deadly qualification, LACKS CONCENTRATION.

Under the circumstances, I claim this slur as a victory.

A less serious trouble in my path was ground school. We studied principles of flight and engineering and navigation, but

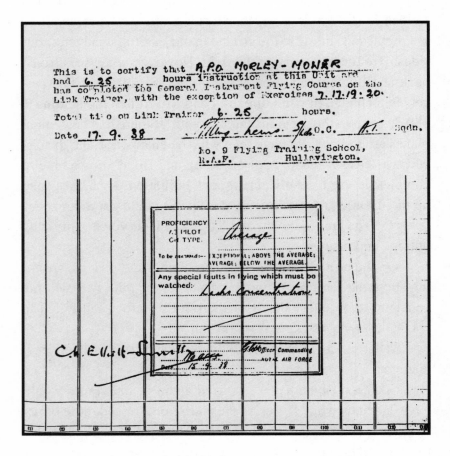

The page from the flying instructor's log book
with the infamous remark, "Lacks concentration."

none of these subjects held my attention. I scraped through the exams as I had done as a boy, with the slimmest margin of error I could calculate. The mystery of flight reduced to thrust and drag and weight and lift dumbed it down in my imagination. The piston engine was a riddle to me, and has remained so to this day. There was an aero engine in one of the classrooms, with its framework cut back to reveal the workings. This was meant to make its function clear to us, but it did not help my condition of invincible ignorance. In the end I had to study hard from the book, memorizing by heart the names and numbers that made no sense in my head.

This inability to understand the simplest mechanical system has dogged me throughout life. Knowing that the part of my brain that dealt with such things was missing, I would write down performance limits of the aircraft I flew—and even then I could not retain them. I can remember being chased by Messerschmitts in a Hawker Hurricane and thinking, "Shall I push the throttle through the 'gate,' to get the extra power?"—and deciding not to do so because I couldn't recall how long the engine would stand the power boost before blowing up!

2

NIGHT FLYING
29th April 1938 to 15th November 1938

"How do you tell your height above the ground if you can't see the ground?" I asked.

"You'll see when we get up there, sir. You have to interpret the lights. It's quite easy. There's nothing to be scared at."

"I'm not scared exactly." But I was.

Sergeant Boyd was sitting on a bench in the locker room performing what was for him a routine task, briefing a student for his first night solo. All the other instructors had been talking earnestly to their students before leaving the hangar to take off. But I wasn't ready to go.

"A light is just a light," I went on. "It could be six feet away or six million miles away."

"You're wasting time, sir. There's no good arguing about it. Let's get this thing over."

Boyd stood up abruptly and reached for his helmet. I followed him out of the dimly lit hangar into the coal black night. As we walked towards the line of parked aircraft the figures of airmen, riggers and fitters, flickered round the machines like ghosts, their faces occasionally showing up in the glow of a wingtip light. The aircraft that had already been started up were an alarming sight. The exhaust stubs, inconspicuous by day, glowed red hot. When the engines were run up against the chocks to test magnetos, sheets of orange and blue flame licked the canvas covered fuselage. It looked as if the fabric would go up in flames and the whole aircraft with it. In the distance the landing flares, a string of kerosene oil lamps that marked the landing path, stood like witches at a midnight sabbath.

Night flying had been my great fear. I used to walk out on to the airfield to watch the senior course—three months ahead of us—at their landing practice. It looked impossibly difficult. The aerodrome was in almost total darkness, every effort having been made to reduce the confusion of electric lights while night flying was in progress. There did not seem to be sufficient illumination for landing. Was there going to be something out there, I wondered, that only perfect eyes could see. Would this be the issue that I couldn't fudge?

We taxied out with three Audaxes in front of us. Throttled back, their engines crackled, popped and burned with showers of sparks alarming the darkness. Incoming aircraft crashed their wheels on the turf, bounced, and took off again with a roar of engine power. You could hear the thud of rubber against grass and the squeezing of tortured oleo legs.[1]

An Aldis light flashed unmistakeably green from somewhere low down beyond the flare path.

"You can take off now," said Boyd quietly, like a trainer handling a nervous horse. "Just keep her straight."

We shot off into the dark. There were very few lights to be seen on the ground except the flickering oil lamps. Other aircraft showed up well against the sky with port and starboard lights

---

[1] Undercarriage struts filled with oil to absorb the shock of the main wheels when they strike the ground.

winking as they flew the circuit. Boyd talked me round and on to the glide path.

"Don't look at the individual flares. Judge your height by the angle they make."

My slightly blurred vision didn't hamper my judgement of angles and I pulled off a whisper of a landing, throttling back gently and finding my wheels on the ground before I expected.

"Very good," said Boyd. "Now you have to do it again."

My second and third landings were not as distinguished as my first, but Boyd sent me solo without further comment. Chalk that one up, I said to myself, settling my secret spectacles under the flap of my helmet, seeing the nightscene in high definition, points of light shining like diamonds in the dark.

The technique of landing an aircraft by night is not to look at the flares directly, as if to search for where the ground is, but to gauge the height by the changing appearance of the lights as you fly forward and downward. I found myself very much at home with this technique, which had an element of pure trust in it. Once the glide path is established the appearance of the flare path changes from instant to instant. As you get closer to the earth the lights flatten out and open up. When they begin to flash past your ears, you know that you are very close. At this point there is a tendency to yank the stick backward and balloon upwards, because you fear colliding with the ground at an ugly angle. This is where faith, or something akin to it, comes in. Everything will be all right provided you don't do anything violent. You have to imagine, rather than see, your height above the ground.

It was a night to remember. April 9th, 1938. Sergeant Boyd was pleased with himself for his handling of the situation.

"You didn't have a thing to worry about," he said. "I knew it all the time."

"I just couldn't see how it could be done till I did it," I explained.

"That's what I was getting at," said Boyd triumphantly.

*   *   *

The aircraft we flew at Hullavington were the Hawker Hart and the Hart variant called the Audax. The Hart was designed in 1926 as a high performance bomber to replace the maid-of-all-work De Havilland 9A, which had been used since 1918 both as a fighter and light bomber. The Hart had a top speed of 184 mph (296 km/h) and for a time in the Thirties it could compete well with contemporary fighters. The front line squadrons were equipped with them until 1937 when the new monoplanes, Whitleys, Blenheims, Battles and Wellesleys came along. As a pure flying machine it was superb, sensitive on the controls and difficult to fly. It had no vices, like some of the earlier types, but taking off and landing were more of an adventure than on the tame little Avro Cadet.

On take-off the Rolls Royce Kestrel engine would exert such a powerful torque that the pilot had to kick on full opposite rudder to keep a straight path over the turf airfield. Landing wasn't easy, because the undercarriage was unyielding. If you panicked, and pulled out of a glide too crudely, it would stall a foot or two above the earth but fail to settle. A slightly ill-judged landing would result in a bucking motion which was humiliating. A real whistler of an arrival was an achievement, a work of art. One small bounce was considered satisfactory. Instructors would sometimes demonstrate their special skills by landing tail up, in the flying position, by exquisite handling of the elevators, holding the wheels down to the grass surface while the wings were still giving some lift. I once sat spellbound behind Boyd as he brought the kite in fast, shook off the excess, speed, and then jammed his main wheels on terra firma as if he had exclusive rights over the laws of nature.

Diary entry: 27th April 1936
    We're now on a series of cross country flights and we're allowed to plan our own sorties. There's a magic land down there and I'm going to fly over all the glory

spots in the west of England. On Monday I flew over Stonehenge, the ring of huge sarsen stones looking neater than they do from the ground. I circled Salisbury Cathedral and then set out southwest to look at the Cerne Abbas Giant. It is cut into the chalk of a whaleback green hillside, and the giant brandishes a club and has an erect penis. Today I flew a long stretch to St Michael's Mount in Cornwall, a Medieval monastery converted into a noble house for the St Aubyn family. It was low tide when I passed overhead and you could see the causeway to the island with a horse and cart crossing back to the mainland. Then a short track north- ward to Tintagel, the ruins of Uther Pendragon's castle on the north Cornwall coast, where we scrambled one dark night when I was fourteen, hoping to see Arthur's ghost.

On 21st May 1938, 1 had a CFI test—a routine check of all students by the Chief Flying Instructor, Squadron Leader Bett. I did pretty well and was particularly elated at pulling off a slithery landing. Riding back to the officers mess on my bicycle I had an accident. The idea of suffering a serious injury on a pedal bike did not occur to me. I was in an excited frame of mind and peddling rapidly. The road from the hangars was crowded with airmen walking back to their quarters. I saw a narrow gap between pedestrians and shot through, only to find a young airman, also on a bicycle, speeding through the same gap. I used violent eva- sive action to starboard, but he went the same way and we col- lided. The impact threw me forward and my left cheek crunched against his handlebar breaking the cheekbone and pushing it into my face.

It was very painful at first and I was walked to Sick Quarters where the station medical officer at once ordered an ambulance to take me to the nearest military hospital at Tidworth on the Salisbury Plain. There I languished for two weeks. Doctors came to see me, prodded and poked the blue and red injury, and did nothing. I was anxious at missing so much flying. We were running up to graduation and I could see myself being held over to the next course—a ghastly delay in my scheme of things. My father came to see me and was distressed at the wreck of my face. He called me 'Ricks,' a pet name from childhood, and worried that I'd never again recover my looks, such as they were. Lying bored and idle in bed, I wrote a four stanza "Ballade of a Broken Face." One stanza can be quoted to show my state of mind.

> With one accord they say, "It looks all right."
> (A sunken cheekbone and a drooping eye)
> Some praise it as a fascinating sight,
> But others with more honest spirits sigh,
> Yet say they like it, but do not know why.
> I'm terribly depressed about the thing.
> It makes me look lopsided, more or less.
> My mouth won't come apart enough to sing.
> I think I'm in a perfect bloody mess.

When I was returned to Hullavington the medical officer. banned me from flying for a further week, because my face was still swollen and dented. Flight Sergeant Boyd was grimly determined that I would pass out on time. I think he believed he'd overcome, by his excellent instruction, my early difficulties with seeing objects clearly, and he was proud of my CFI test, which reflected credit on himself.

"You've had a nasty knock there," he said. "You look pretty awful. But now we have to get a lot of things done. We have ten exercises to do to catch up with the others."

The depression of my left cheek is still with me. I notice it while shaving, one cheek a millimetre or so below the other. When I play golf the sun hits and reddens them unequally, so that one apple-red blob of flesh is clearly seen to be out of position under my left eye. Few people notice it, though. I have pointed it out to my wives, close relatives and friends, recounting the tragic event, but they have not been impressed.

Though night landings had ceased to be a terror to me, the night cross-country was an important event, the nearest I had yet been to launching out into the unknown. It was the last hurdle before graduation. Hawker Harts had no radios. Once airborne we were alone in the blackness over England and dependent on the few skills acquired from our instructors. If anything went wrong, there was no one to appeal to. If we were lost the only thing to do was to throttle back, conserve fuel, and hope to blunder across an airfield that had not closed down for the night.

Strapped to one knee was the log on which, in the roar and confusion of the cockpit, we would record the time of departure, the airspeed maintained and any changes of course. On the other knee was the heavy navigational calculator for working out the windspeed, once the drift of the aircraft from its planned track had been observed. How would we recognize the unfamiliar lights of towns we'd never seen from the air?

"Bristol is a big white city," said Boyd. "Bath is orange coloured but smaller. If you can remember that you won't confuse them."

July 13, 1938, was a cloudless night, no doubt specially chosen to give students as little trouble as possible. We had to fly a simple triangular course, map reading our way round and making the necessary changes of heading to arrive overhead at the turning points. There were few lights to be seen in the countryside around Hullavington and it required an effort to drag myself away from the security of the flare path. Fifteen minutes from setting course I saw in the distance, as Boyd predicted, an orange city. As I approached I could see, by the way a crescent of street lamps curved beneath me, that it was built on a hill. It was Bath. Beyond it, spread out from north to south as a line of brightness, was

Bristol; an electric blue city, delineated sharply by the coastline and the dark sea beyond.

In an open cockpit anything loose, like a map not firmly grasped, can be sucked out and lost forever. To make log entries the map had to be stowed and the stick transferred to the left hand to free the right hand for writing. One's head had to be lowered to see the log in the dimness of the internal cockpit lights. Ideally the aircraft would proceed steadily while the scribbling was being done. In practice, when one looked up a wing had dropped, the airspeed had built up, and the aircraft was thirty degrees off course! But there was no one to observe me going through these struggles. I arrived over Hullavington feeling that I had conquered the empire of the night. Dark as it was, the shape of Malmesbury Abbey could be distinguished against the street lights of the little town. It was very comforting. I didn't want to come in. I flew around for twenty minutes, looking at the darkened earth, enjoying the strangeness of flying through the star-filled sky.

> Diary entry: 15th September 1938
> Everyone's talking about where we'll be sent after passing out. Also what kites we'll be flying. My worst fear is to go to some tame squadron in East Anglia, fifty miles from London. This is my chance to get half-way round the world without having to pay the fare, and I'd hate to miss it. They told us to list our prefer-ences and I put down flying boats as number one, be-cause nearly all the boat squadrons are overseas. Num-ber two Hong Kong, because it is a long distance from England. Number three India, because there are lots of squadrons in India and no one else wants to go there.

The influence behind my first choice was Flight Lieutenant Trewick, a middle-aged ex-pilot who was performing some administrative duty in station headquarters. On dining-in nights, when all the officers were required to attend a ritual meal dressed in mess kit—tight blue trousers over patent leather boots, stiff shirts, bum freezers and medals (for those who had any)—he would become expansive with booze and talk obsessively of the boats. I loved to hear his stories of flying out of Rangoon or Singapore, crossing the Pacific waters to refuel by the palm green shores of atolls, where the natives paddled drums of petrol to the floating craft in their outrigger canoes. "A flying boat," he used to say, "is a wondrous thing," a world unto itself beyond the reach of boring administrators, a flying island like Swift's Laputa, with its own kitchen from which delicious steaks could be served to the crew during long ocean voyages..

Hong Kong was my second choice because a squadron of Gloster Gladiators the most advanced biplane fighter, was stationed there. It was as far away from England that you could go, the mysterious East to boot, and Chinese junks with square sails and ladies with split skirts. I had no real chance, with my qualified average category, but I couldn't resist putting it down. After all, my luck had held this far. Finally, India. I knew nothing about India, but my best friend from school, Patrick Biggie, had been accepted for a commission in the Indian Police and I would have companionship on adventurous holidays in the Himalayas. I was posted to No. 27 Squadron, Kohat, India, (now Pakistan) and I was happy when the news came through.

Cliff Cooper, the chiropractor, who of course was bound for a flying boat squadron, commiserated with me as we stood before the notice board in the mess.

"You'll be flying Wapitis, man! The most outdated kite in the service. That's really going back into the past. They haven't even got brakes!"

"Neither have flying boats!"

I wanted to go back into the past. The more primitive the better. If it wasn't to be outriggers paddling from remote Pacific islands, it might be coolies in white turbans performing similar tasks at the tiny landing grounds that linked the deserts of Arabia with the Great Sind Desert. I was well pleased with my lot.

Our passing out parade was in the third week of September 1938. The RAF is admirably low key about such things. The station band played "Colonel Bogey" and the station commander made a brief speech congratulating the survivors, but there was no nonsense, like pinning wings on our empty breasts. We just had them sewn on professionally and turned up for the parade.

Billy Bowden was a Canadian. His father had married an English girl and then perished on the Western Front. So Billy had been raised in England and had a nice upper class British accent. But he was a Canadian. You always had to remember that. We had become friends on the troopship *SS Neuralia* which took us from Southampton in southern England to Bombay in southern India. We filled the empty days on shipboard by talking about flying and girls. Our conversations about flying were well informed, for we had both read the literature of early flight. Our favourites were *Sagittarius Rising* by Cecil Lewis, the record of a pilot's life on the Western Front, and Antoine de St Exupery's *Night Flight* and *Wind, Sand and Stars*, accounts by a gifted writer of early commercial aviation in South America and North Africa. We knew nothing about girls, but there were a half a dozen on board, daughters of officers posted or returning to India after leave in England. We encountered them walking the boat deck, sitting enticingly on deck chairs with their mothers, at table with both parents in the first-class dining room, and thrillingly close while negotiating the narrow gangways of the ship. Billy was short of stature and didn't fancy his chances in competition with fifty other junior officers all pursuing the same girls; but he egged me on to chase Desiree Tyrrell, a seventeen-year-old whose first name was prophetic of her unique position on the troopship. Her family was returning to Jubbulpore, a city in Central India which figured in my dreams for a couple of years afterwards.

She was not a specially pretty girl, but she had wide-spaced eyes, a generous mouth, and her small waist accentuated the sensual shape of her hips. Her legs were long but too muscular for beauty. She moved about vivaciously in a series of white dresses as the ship drove steadily through the Mediterranean, the Suez Canal and the Indian Ocean. She played deck tennis, swam in the ship's pool and horsed around—she was still a youngster, straight from boarding school, self-contained one moment, sprawling out the next. We got on well together, and I should have moved farther ahead with her than I did, but a crowd of subalterns followed her around as if she were a movie star. On two occasions I persuaded her to walk out of a dance on to the boat deck, and we kissed as the black sea rushed beneath us. I wanted to blurt out something irrevocable, like, "I love you. Marry me." But I was stopped by the thought of my half-formed plan to climb the Hindu Kush and walk to Samarkand. After the intimacy and excitement of the kissing I couldn't find anything to say. There seemed to be no words I could use between, "I love you," which was too much, and, "I did enjoy our last dance," which was too little. At the end of the voyage we still did not know one another and I was one of a dozen men who had kissed her on the boat deck.

At Port Said we went ashore. From the early morning brown Egyptian boys had been diving for coins, thrown into the water by passengers at the rails. I found this very sad and was glad to get away. Billy and I were not interested in shopping. We wanted adventure. Taking the first horse and buggy available we set off across the town. Our driver, a round faced man with a red tarboosh on his shaven head, did not speak any English. Soon we were jogging down broad modern streets. There was a tramway system, a few automobiles, and a European air about the office buildings and department stores. Elegantly dressed men and women crowded the pavements.

Without consulting us, the driver turned down a side street, and we were soon making our way through narrow, cobbled alleys, with low flat-roofed houses on either side. It was a foreign looking world and fascinating to our unjaded eyes. Progress was slowed by groups of people in white Egyptian robes buying fruit and vegetables from stalls set out in the street. We stopped in front of a large ugly building, imposing in comparison to its neighbours. The driver asked for his fare. This was, apparently, the destination he had chosen for us. We paid him off and mounted the broad steps to the double door.

The vestibule was huge and empty with a balcony running along the back wall. A servant ran off and in a minute a fat lady, dressed in black satin with a rope of pearls round her neck, waddled in. She seemed very pleased to see us.

"Ah," she said. "Nize young men. I have ispecial girl for you."

She ushered us to a settee where we sat bolt upright, our hats on our knees. She clapped her hands, and a bell sounded upstairs. In a minute twenty girls had turned out for our inspection. They were in various stages of undress, mostly thin and unattractive. They smiled and gestured like marionettes. Some of them descended the stairs and lined up, posing in inviting attitudes. Others leaned over the balcony and sang out obscene phrases in English. Some of them had negroid features but most had the beaky, long-necked look one associates with southern Italy. Two very young and frightened looking blondes stood, hand-in-hand, directly in front of us.

"You can choose one of zeez," she announced in a commanding tone.

All I could think of was escape. It was sadder than those little boys diving for coins in the dirty water of the harbour.

I looked at Billy. He was blushing to the roots of his hair. Our eyes met and there was no doubt remaining.

We grabbed our hats and ran.

3

THE WILD FRONTIER
24th November 1938, to 1st March 1939

The Northwest Frontier Province, to which I had been sent as a humble servant of the Raj, was an ungovernable region. This fact was concealed from those living in peaceable areas, such as Kohat, where 27 Squadron was located. It would have been rash to leave aircraft out on the square grass airfield at night, and they were always wheeled into the green painted hangars, locked, and guarded. But bullets did not fly here, roads were never blocked in order to ambush convoys or to harm innocent civilians. Order and civilization prevailed in the British cantonment. The bungalows of the married officers, with servants quarters and stables attached, were as safe as if they were on the Salisbury Plain. The officers messes of the army regiments, the Royal Air Force and the Indian cavalry stood in their own grounds and resembled country clubs, where the best of food and drink were at hand, and servants were at beck and call at all times. At the fringes of these estates, with their swimming pools, tennis courts and the obligatory high wall of the squash courts, were extensive playing fields for cricket, soccer and polo.

This rather phoney and local tranquillity had been achieved by separating the tribal areas from the rest of the province. In these troubled areas the two main tribes, the Wazirs and the Mahsuds, lived as they had done for centuries, in a state of perpetual minor warfare. Their menfolk walked like warriors and held their heads high, biblical garments giving them an extra dignity. I got the impression, as my bearer (personal servant) talked of his native village in the Ahmadzai, that his brothers would have enjoyed themselves shooting down my aeroplane, blowing up my military transport and slitting my throat rather than pressing my trousers, setting out my clothes, and attending my daily bath with outstretched towel. This dichotomy ran through every aspect of life on the frontier. The tribes hated the British but joined the army and became servants for the pay. The British admired their independent spirit.

The ungovernability of the Pashtu-speaking tribes had been demonstrated during the 19th century, when expansion of the empire had been on Britain's agenda. In 1842, General Elphinstone's army attempted to conquer Afghanistan but was cut to pieces in the tragic retreat from Kabul, a single survivor, Dr William Brydon, made his way to the comparative safety of Jalalabad. The Durand Line, a border negotiated between British India and Afghanistan, established an apparently sensible frontier. It followed a mountain range and was theoretically defensible, but it made no sense to the Wazirs, who felt themselves to be Afghans rather than Indians, and whose villages and grazing grounds were on both sides of the range.

The newly created state of Pakistan has inherited the problem which we created. The same Pathans who once harrassed us were recently calling themselves 'freedom fighters' and demanding a separate state to be called 'Pushtunistan.' From 1961 to 1963 the Pakistan army sustained severe casualties as marauding tribesmen invaded and looted the peaceful plains. Nowadays, my Pakistani friends tell me, the tribal areas are left to themselves,

The Northwest Frontier Province showing the forts,
tribal locations, and areas flown over by the author.
Courtesy: Terrence Haney.

and are recognized as being beyond the reach of the law. In other words, everything is as it was before the British came meddling.

When I arrived by the Frontier Mail at Kohat railway station in November 1938, the region was in an uproar. The trouble had begun in 1936 when the Bannu Brigade was ambushed at Biche Kaskai in the Tochi valley and suffered 131 casualties. It was an unusually large-scale and well-organized ambush and it signalled the arrival on the scene of a tribal leader called the Faqir of Ipi, who continued to cause trouble into the 1950s. The British response was to punish those responsible by denying them traditional grazing areas. But before this point was reached every kind of stick and carrot diplomacy was used. Effective sanctions were feeble because the tribal leaders knew that the League of Nations' rules banned direct military action.

The punishment was called 'proscription.' A tribal grazing ground was chosen—either because it was close to a road that had been ambushed, or the assailants were known to graze their cattle in that area—and it would be proscribed, or forbidden to be used. Leaflets would be dropped from the air setting out the conditions, and giving time for the evacuation of people and cattle. It was enforced by constant surveillance from the air. Any beasts that had been left behind could be killed.

There was an uneasy relationship between the political agents and the military. The P.A.'s were government civilians, acknowledged experts on the area, who tended to identify strongly with 'their,' tribesmen, admired their independance and martial vigour, and did everything to keep the army and the air force out of the equation. But at a certain level of atrocity the Indian government would declare martial law, leaving the P.A.'s wringing their hands. Incidents were bound to happen.

North Waziristan could be described as the valley of the Tochi River. Along the banks of this river a string of mud and brick forts, garrisoned by Tochi Scouts, a local militia, kept the roads open. The roads were essential because the Bannu Brigade, the largest British military force in the province, had to be able to reinforce its remote outpost at Razmak, a base high up on the range close to the Afghan border.

Johnny Darwen was the commander of 'C' Flight, to which Billy and I were assigned. During the Second World War he made a considerable name for himself as a ferocious fighter and ground attack pilot. In 1940 he was dining with his newly wed wife in the Cafe de Paris in London when a bomb fell, destroying the building and killing his wife beside him. Afterwards he went on a much decorated rampage against the Germans, which ended with his death on a Beaufighter raid on northern Italy in 1944. When I knew him he was a couple of years younger, short of stature but brilliantly goodlooking in the Ray Milland style of masculine beauty. He was a regular officer, a Cranwell boy,[1] and a strict disciplinarian.

I was talking to Billy Bowden at the entrance of the hangar, staring longingly at the Westland Wapitis we were soon to fly. It was a cold December day and we had turned up the collars of our thick Crombie greatcoats, and had put our hands in our pockets. This was a serious mistake. We may have thought we looked like Russian princes in Tolstoy's *War and Peace*, but we were swiftly disillusioned. Johnny Darwen strode towards us and in a loud voice, icy with contempt, said, "Take your hands out of your pockets." All the airmen working on the machines, the flight sergeant at his hangar desk and the coolies waiting to push out the remaining aircraft heard the order and stared at us.

"And turn down your greatcoat collars. Never put your hands in your pockets while wearing His Majesty's uniform. You are not advertisments for de Rezske cigarettes. You are Royal Air Force officers."

---

[1] Royal Air Force College, Cranwell, in Lincolnshire, is the equivalent of Sandhurst for the British Army or West Point for the U.S. Army.

above: Billy Bowden *(l.)* and the author at Kohat, December 1939.
below: The 27th Squadron hanger at Kohat, India, 1938 with a 31
Squadron Valentia parked in front. Note the Squadron crest on the
roof.

This was our introduction to 27 Squadron, and not an auspicious one. In my subsequent thirty-one years in the air force I never once put my hands into the pockets of my greatcoat or turned up my wide beautiful Crombie collar. Much attention was given to dressing up in those days. Dinner jackets were worn every night except weekends, when sports jackets were acceptable wear. Dining-in night was on Thursday, a formal get together of all officers in full mess kit, dull and ritualistic. There was a form for everything. When to stand, when to sit, don't light up before the C.O., who follows whom into the dining room. The port circulated after dinner. Awful stuff! I had no idea what port could be like until I took 224 Squadron to Lisbon on a goodwill visit in 1951, and the British port producers filled our four-engined Shackletons with nectar of the gods.

Guest nights were less frequent, perhaps every two months. On these occasions officers from the infantry, gunner and cavalry regiments were invited. I remember being astounded at the splendour of the cavalrymen, with chain mail on their epaulettes, broad golden stripes down their trouser legs and scarlet cummerbunds. Darwen gave us strict instructions as to our behaviour.

"Arrive early and wait until the mess president arrives. He will be a senior flight lieutenant. I am president tonight. Come up to me and say good evening, and then retire to some obscure section of the anteroom. Do not, under any circumstances, stand in front of the fireplace. That is for the C.O. and the senior officers, which does not at present include you. When the station commander arrives and orders a drink, you may order a drink. Speak when you are spoken to. Otherwise be attentive and follow the lead of others."

Billy and I turned up in time for the Christmas guest night, a grand affair attended by the brigadier, the brigade major and other dignitaries. After dinner were the obligatory rough games. The senior flight lieutenants, Darwen and Selkirk, took off their jackets and flung them down. Their ties and collars followed. We obediently did likewise. They called up the heaviest of us to form a human base and sent middleweights, such as myself, to climb over the phalanx of flesh to form a pyramid. Nimbler officers jumped up and were assisted to the top of the pile of bodies. Darwen himself was the last to clamber up, shouting for lift and support. Twice the effort failed, and we all came tumbling down. At the third attempt the wobbly pyramid held up for a few seconds while Johnny placed a foot on the ceiling. The distinguished guests and the station commander applauded our efforts; but a half an hour later they had drifted off and the singing of lewd songs began—"Eskimo Nell," "The Ball of Kerrymuir," and "The Harlot of Jerusalem." These were standard fare on guest nights, but a new song with an ironically jolly tune intrigued me. It told of the sad fate of a pilot who set out over Waziristan, suffered an engine failure, and was forced to land in tribal territory. The refrain was troubling.

> No balls at all
> No balls at all
> When your engine cuts out you'll have
> No balls at all.

"What's that about?" I exclaimed, breaking the rule by speaking before I was spoken to. But Darwen had a drink taken, as the Irish say. His eyes lit up at the prospect of instructing one of his minions.

"What you fellows don't realize," he said, "is that the Wazirs are a tough bunch. Not long ago an army officer was captured during a skirmish. The next day his skin was found laid out on a rock near his regimental headquarters. If they can get hold of you, they'll remove your private parts and sew them in your mouth. If they flay you, like they flayed the army chap, they'll probably do it while you're still alive and screaming. You can't afford to get an engine failure over tribal territory unless you want to come home in small pieces. Checking your engine for a magneto drop is serious business up here. You're not flying over the Home Counties."

"It's hard to believe," I said.

"Well, they're in the Middle Ages. The English used to hang, draw and quarter traitors on Tyburn Hill, and these people don't see anything wrong with torturing their enemies to death. We are their enemies. We drop bombs on them and otherwise interfere with their lives. They don't have any mercy for us. The women do most of the torturing. Death of a thousand cuts. They cut off bits and pieces, eylids, nose, nipples. Then they stick thorns into the open wounds to make it worse. Very artistic. It's well documented. That's why we wear goolie chits."

I had not fully realized the significance of the piece of official paper, signed by the governor of the province, and which I was advised to keep on my person at all times. It was called a goolie chit, because the Urdu word for ball is *gholi*. I vaguely understood that it offered a reward for not violating my body in the traditional fashion. (Example on following page.)[2]

---

[2] An English translation of the notice to be carried by all air force pilots flying over Tribal Territory. The message is printed in Pashtu on the left and Urdu on the right:

HIS EXCELLENCY THE GOVERNOR
OF
THE NORTHWEST FRONTIER PROVINCE
The bearer of this letter is on official duty with the air force and is under the protection of the Indian government. He should be well treated and be immediately and safely brought to the nearest government post. A reward is offered if this is done. The government will severely punish any attempt to harm him.
SIGNATURE OF GOVERNOR

GOVERNOR OF THE NORTHWEST FRONTIER PROVINCE

(This document is the property of Wing Commander G.W. Topliss and has kindly been provided by him.)

A goolie chit, which pilots were to carry
whenever flying over enemy territory.

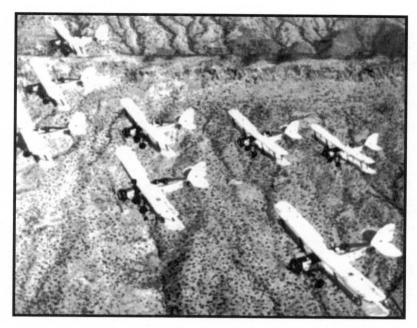

above: 27 Squadron flying Westland Wapitis with DH9A wings in formation over the hills near Kohat in early 1939.   *below*: 'C' Flight in formation over Kohat, Johnny Darwen, Logger Powley, and Freddie Lambert flying.

"But no goolie chit will save you" Darwen went on cheer-fully. "They have all sorts of nice ways of killing you off. A soldier taken in an ambush was finished off by having his mouth fixed open by a stick. Then all the women used him as a lavatory until he drowned. Death by choking is one of their milder remedies. Not a fitting end for tender lads like you and Bowden. Pilot offic-ers on probation!"

A shout of laughter went up at that. Johnny Darwen's raised voice had attracted a group of old timers, eager to tell even more frightful stories, proving that they were wise in the ways of the wild frontier. This was the second, but certainly not the last of my culture shocks. Later on a very pleasant army captain, who'd been with the Bannu Brigade, told me about the khassadars, ineffective government-funded police force of tribesmen who were meant to preserve law and order, but in fact colluded with their brothers in mayhem. And about the curious way the tribesmen would join up in the Indian army and serve loyally all over the world for their pay; then return to their villages to shoot up British convoys. It was said that some of these confused ex-soldiers applied for fron-tier medals, to add to their collection of legitimate medals, not fully aware that they were fighting on the other side. This kind of thought process is only explicable in the context of an area that has been continuously at war since the dawn of history. Family feuds, lasting through centuries, account for much of it. But the. Wazirs have an ethos of warfare, like the heroes of Homer. I could imagine Alexander the Great, jingling down the Tochi Val-ley and making camp at nightfall. These people would watch him all day from behind large rocks, and then pick off stragglers or attack just after dark for booty. If an army showed any real weak-ness it would be wiped out to the last man, as General Elphinstone discovered to his grief.

Diary entry: 23rd January 1939
Heard a fantastic tale yesterday. I was in the Kohat

Club library, looking for something on the history of India. A fairly old man was sitting there. I think he's a judge in the I.C.S. [Indian Civil Service] Seeing me among the histories, he held forth for twenty minutes on the current situation in the province. Nothing I didn't know, except this. The tribesmen know that we are bound by the League of Nations ban on the killing of civilians, and they've devised a method of claiming that we do. They'll tie an old woman across the back of a sturdy sheep and drive the animal into a proscription area, hoping one of our pilots will attack. Then they bring in the body of the old lady, filled with our .303 bullets, and demand a monetary settlement. It's hard to believe. But so many things here are hard to believe.

I reported this conversation to Johnny Darwen.

"I believe that was done," he said. "Just once. But it's a year or so ago. It made a great stir at the time. The political agents paid up, but let the tribal leaders, the maliks, know that it wasn't going to work a second time. It's a serious matter to kill anyone on the ground, though. We'll be starting ops from Miramshah in a few days. My advice is, if you see a Wazir in the proscription area, leave him alone. Fly back and report it. We're unpopular enough as it is."

I soon discovered that everyone hero-worshipped the Tochi Scouts. They were the glamour boys of the frontier. The more I learned about them the weirder and more admirable they seemed. For one thing they were supported by civil, not military, funds. This put them under the direct control of the political officers, who used them to more subtle effect. Halfway between a commando and an eccentric police force, they were recruited from the tribes, but no Tochi Scout was allowed to serve in his own area. Most of them were Mahsuds from the south, or men from Gilgit in the north. The officers were British, seconded from the Indian Army regiments, with one or two Indians thrown in. They were an interesting bunch, attracted to the romance of commanding 250 men in an isolated fort on the Tochi River that looked as if it had been constructed for a movie set on the French Foreign Legion. They were armed only with rifles, and would run (never walk) up to fifty miles a day on a *gasht*, or patrol. When they were called out to respond to an emergency, such as an ambush, or to arrest a malik who was harbouring outlaws, it was called a *barampta*. They always carried their own rudimentary supplies of food with them, and some stretchers for the wounded. It was a job for a hero who was also an athlete, and I never heard anything but praise for their effectiveness. Johnny Darwen said the last word on that, too.

"Aeroplanes are not the answer to governing the province. It's good fun for us, but bad politics. They think being bombed is unfair. After all, they have no aircraft to strike back with. But they don't resent the Tochis at all. They love the Tochis. Everyone loves the Tochis."

One of the strange and unexpected bonuses of being on the Afghan border was the pitiless sun that burned down on bare rock and humans alike for most of the year. During the hours of daylight everyone wore tinted glasses when out of doors. All pilots were issued with dark lensed flying goggles, and most pilots used them. I always flew in my sunglasses, which looked quite natural and which no one suspected of having corrected lenses. My remaining concern was that I would fail the eye test for a routine annual medical exam, but this threat also disappeared. When the war broke out in September 1939 annual medicals were dropped, to my immense relief. Not until the war was over, when I had to appeal to the monarch to retain my flying category, did this issue return.

4

THE UNEXPLODED BOMB
8th March 1939 to 13th March 1939

My rear gunner was Corporal Rollo, a heavily muscled blond fellow with lots of experience in the air. I could tell that he didn't appreciate going up with a young pilot straight out of flying school. On 8th March, at about nine in the morning, we walked together, toting our parachutes, through the huge gates of Miramshah Fort to where Wapiti K1258 sat in a line of aircraft facing into wind. The Westland Wapiti had been designed in 1927 to use up spare parts of the De Havilland 9A, an aircraft which had become famous in the last year of World War I. It had the same wood-and-wire look as the Sopwith Camel and the Avro 504. I was thrilled to be flying a machine so similar to those once flown by heroes of the Royal Flying Corps. It had two open cockpits, a radial engine, and was equipped with a tailwheel but no brakes.

The racks under each wing of the Wapiti already had bombs suspended. Two airmen were in attendance to get it started. Rollo bustled about doing the aircraft checks after me. If he was going to fly with an idiot who had less than a hundred hours in the air, he was going to make sure that all the locknuts were secure. I had peered rather vaguely under the fuselage, but he grasped the crossbracing wires of the fixed undercarriage and shook them. He ran his large competent hands along the leading edges of the wings, feeling for the adherence of some fabric repair patches. Moving back, he checked that the ailerons swung freely on their hinges. Then he shook them—much more roughly than I had done—to make sure they were properly mounted. He walked to the tail and carried out the same procedure on the more massive surfaces of the rudder and elevators. He was a rigger and only a part-time air gunner. This was his routine job. It is possible that he wouldn't have trusted any pilot to do his checks correctly, but I felt that his performance was directed at me. Then he climbed into the rear cockpit and swung his Lewis gun around. I felt his anxiety and was sorry for him, having to fly with me over the Madda Khel.

I pulled the safety pins out of the four 24-pound bombs and the two 112-pound bombs that hung from racks beneath the wings. Rollo was arranging the ammunition belt so that it fed smoothly into his gun. I climbed into the front cockpit, strapped myself in, and signalled to the airman to swing the propeller.

"Switches off. Suck in," he shouted.

I checked my magneto switches down.

"Switches off," I said.

He turned the prop round three times by hand. I could hear the cylinders wheezing as the engine turned over.

"Ready to go. Switches on."

I switched on and opened my throttle one third, as I had been taught. The airman reached up, leaned a little on the prop blade, testing it. Then he linked up with two other airmen who were necessary to provide the extra power. The other method of starting was to use the low geared starting handles, an airman winding away on either side. Both methods were used, but Wapitis were always tricky to start. This time it coughed and fired. When the prop was chunking around merrily I throttled back to warm up the engine gradually.

I took off, leaving a plume of yellow dust in my wake, turned on the climb and circled the field. The red bulk of the fort squatted below my port wing. It was constructed of mud and brick, like any fortified village in the area, and castellated like a Crusader castle. A conical hill overlooked the scene. At night the local tribesmen would climb this eminence and fire shots into the fort with their out-of-date rifles. At nightfall all the aircraft were wheeled into the courtyard for protection, and the high metal gates were locked against intruders.

To the north the great mountain range stretched, fold on fold. In the dry air of Waziristan the eye picks up shapes in exaggerated definition. Shadows were black in the gullies, little sign of vegetation on the bare hillsides, the outlines crisp and austere. The village of Miramshah stood on the Tochi River a mile from the fort, shining white in an oasis of green fields. Everything looked closer than it really was. I could see the Madda Khel clearly, though it would take me fifteen minutes to fly there and begin my sortie.

A month previously the Madda Khel Wazirs had descended from their high mountains, entered the provincial town of Bannu and looted the bazaar, kidnapping two Hindu maidens and taking them back into tribal territory. The government protest was answered by an emissary of the Faqir of Ipi, who made it known that the girls had been converted to Islam and had no interest in returning to their parents. There was talk of *Jihad*, or Holy War, if the matter was pursued. That was the end of the negotiation and a proscription was laid on.

On our first pass over the area Rollo saw a camel. It was tethered to a stake beside a square building that had castellations like a fort. There was nothing unusual about that. Some of the villages were made up entirely of fortified houses, sometimes protected by an outer wall. This particular valley, however, had few dwellings. It was an area for grazing and most of the buildings were for temporary shelter only. I didn't want to kill this camel. Why had it been left behind? Perhaps it had been too sick or too

above: Wapitis at Miramshah. The dust clouds in back are a result of running up the planes. *below*: Miramshah Fort in the Tochi River Valley. The airfield is top left.

old to travel. Rollo, the veteran of many proscription sorties, gave the matter no consideration. He at once prepared to fire. We were at about two thousand feet above the floor of the valley. It was a cool cloudless day. The scene was idyllic. The great red-brown hills. The tiny patches of green cultivation near the humble mud dwellings. The Tochi River curling in the distance.

Rollo shouted through the speaking tubes. "Go down to a thousand feet, sir."

"Right."

I throttled back and glided towards the standing camel. I could see it moving around. I lowered my port wing to give him a clear sight of his target and he opened up with his gun. It made a terrible racket, almost drowning out the noise of the engine. I could see the bullets hitting the earth twenty feet short and then running up to and hitting the beast, kicking up dust beyond it. It fell down and struggled to its feet again, its legs splayed, tossing its head in pain.

I made another pass, this time lower down. Rollo was a good shot and he once again hit the camel which fell over and lay still.

"Good shot," I yelled. "I think you killed him."

Rollo shouted something back at me. In the open cockpit the slipstream carried his voice away. He was busy managing his gun and had not spoken directly into the tube. I climbed up to begin the process of getting rid of my bombs. There was a tower to the north of the area which had already been substantially destroyed, either by other pilots or by natural dilapidation. It stood on the edge of a cliff and was an ideal target for dive bombing. From time to time I glanced at the recumbant camel, imagining that it had moved.

It was moving!

"The camel's not dead," I bellowed. "I'll take you down lower this time. Pump it full of lead. The poor bastard."

"Ready to fire, sir."

I glided towards the courtyard, fascinated by the twitching camel and the excess of detail at close range. The rough wooden door of the building, which looked more like a cattle shed as one approached, was open, revealing a dark interior. There was a well, neatly circumscribed by a mud brick wall. It was an illustration from the Bible. Jesus meets the woman at the well.

"You're too low, get higher." Rollo's voice in the wind.

A moment later he opened up at the camel. As I watched the rounds thumping into its carcase I saw a flash of white across the battlements of the barn. Rollo had seen it, too.

"Climb away. Did you see that Wazir?"

"Yes."

"You were much too low, sir. He was probably firing on us. Don't ever go as low as that."

I climbed to four thousand feet. The camel had not stirred. The man had disappeared. Rollo was upset with me and justifiably so.

What should I do now?

Bomb the building? Screech around at low level looking for the man? Don't be crazy! Go home and forget about the whole thing? Above all, don't kill a human being.

I wished Rollo, that Ancient Mariner in the cockpit behind me, that coldblooded murderer of innocent nature, were somewhere else. He knew everything and I knew nothing. All he cared about was the safety of his own skin, apparently. I had gone down low to save the camel some of his terminal agony and Rollo fussed about the Wazir hiding in the cattle shed who might or might not have been shooting at us. I suppose he'll put it all down in the report, and Johnny Darwen will say I did everything wrong. That I put one of His Majesty's Wapitis in jeopardy, and risked the life of Rollo. Hell!

I flew back to the tower on the cliff. The bombing, thank God, wasn't Rollo's business. The technique for dive bombing was to pass directly over the target, throttle back and pull the nose up sharply until the airspeed was within 20 mph of the stall. At this point full rudder is applied. It was called a stalled turn. With the nose pointing vertically upwards at low speed, the rudder wheels the aircraft elegantly on its axis to a position heading vertically downwards. If you have judged it correctly you should be looking straight down at your target. On my first attack the tower was not close enough, but I decided to drop the bomb anyway. I hoped to hit it by pulling out of my dive slightly early and throwing it forward. I had selected the 112-pound bomb on the port wing. Climbing and turning I could see no explosion on the ground. I looked under the wing. The bomb was gone.

"Did you see that bomb explode?"

"No, sir."

"We must have missed it," I said.

"Couldn't have missed it. There's no smoke. It's an unexploded bomb. Better mark its position on your map."

I fished out my map from the pocket of my flying suit and did my best to locate the position of the tower on the rather featureless plateau. The other bombs went off satisfactorily, though I didn't succeed in hitting the tower. I had been upset by the incident of the camel and the bomb not exploding capped it. I flew back disconsolately, feeling in a vague way that I had failed to deliver the goods.

'Shackels' Majumdar was the army liaison officer at Miramshah that season. He was a charming Hindu officer from one of the Indian cavalry regiments. He played polo, drank whiskey and joined in enthusiastically in the rough-house games on dining-in nights. Shackels had been at Harrow and he spoke English without a trace of Indian accent. After my camel-slaying sortie he debriefed me, and I was obliged to explain to him what had happened. He approved the shooting of the camel. He noted that all of the inhabitants had not fled the area.

above: Inside Miramshah Fort, 1939. The castellated fort wall is visible in the background.   *below*: Another view from inside the Fort.

"I am afraid one of my bombs didn't explode," I explained anxiously. "I marked it on my map as accurately as I could. I'll give you the co-ordinates."

"That's very good," said Shackels encouragingly, and wrote down the map references.

"We don't have to find the bombs after the show is over, at least I hope not," I added. "The pinpoint is only approximate because neither Rollo nor myself saw the thing land."

Shackels laughed. "We'll have to see," he said. "We'll have to see."

I didn't see what there was to laugh at and I couldn't interpret his tone.

Late that afternoon I was summoned to the flight commander's office, located in the courtyard close to where the aeroplanes stood at night. It was a tent with walls six feet in height and sandbagged to absorb stray rifle fire. Johnny Darwen, the last man I wanted to see on this tricky subject, had my report in front of him. He had a worried expression on his handsome face.

"I'm afraid we need a more detailed account of this unexploded bomb," he said grimly. "There have been two incidents already. Bowden had one today. The Political Agent is raising hell. He's having a palaver tonight and will blame the air force if one of his Wazirs is accidentally hurt."

The Political Agent for North Waziristan. Major E.H. Cobb, was a large man of about forty who moved clumsily and whose gestures were awkward and embarrassed. Miramshah was his base and we would see him striding around dressed in baggy drill trousers, a much worn sports coat and a battered trilby hat. He had briefed us in his own ample quarters directly after our arrival. I took extensive notes in my diary.

"I'll be frank with you," he had said. "Half the trouble we've had recently has been due to the provocation of the army. The Wazirs are a proud lot, and we have to remember that they'll be living in this country when everyone's forgotten about British rule.

They consider themselves Afghans, though. They don't have any allegiance to India or the Badshah."

"Who's the Badshah?" I whispered to an army officer who was sitting next to me.

"King of Afghanistan," he whispered back.

"The present trouble," the P.A. went on, "is a direct response to our blundering and insensitive army movements. The bloody army insists on using the tribal areas as a training ground. We have 28,000 soldiers here! Quite unnecessary! Only last week the Razmak Brigade sent out a column and lost eleven men to snipers."

He talked on for half an hour about the history of British attempts to rule the troubled province, and then turned to the subject of the Faqir of Ipi.

"The Faqir has the complete loyalty of all Afghans on both sides of the border. They are fanatically religious Muslims and he is demanding what they have always asked for, a separate Islamic republic. Our benighted government, instead of going easy on the religious issue, which they can't possibly win, has sent solemn instructions to the maliks to hand the Faqir over for punishment. The absurdity of that can't be exaggerated. No malik would ever do such a thing, nor would his people let him. Behaving in this foolish fashion simply puts a moral weapon in the hands of our enemies."

"How are we going to get peace on the frontier?" someone asked.

"In my view we should use some judicious bribery," the P.A. answered. "I know it may sound strange to some of you chaps, but bribery is the only thing that really works here. The problem is that the Badshah's money is worth ten times ours. But in this case there is no conflict between the Badshah and ourselves. The last thing we need to do is to send out forces to provoke more incidents."

The P.A.'s second palaver, which did indeed take place that night, was not attended by the junior officers. As far as I remember his audience was confined to Johnny Darwen and Shackels Majumdar. Shackels came to my room after it was over and told me the P.A. had been discomforted at the report of unexploded bombs and had ordered out the Tochi Scouts to render them harmless.

The commander of the Tochis at Miramshah was a big, slack-jawed Indian Army officer called 'Loppy' Lerwill. He had a unique reputation in the fort and was the authority on what could be done in the tribal area.

"Loppy doesn't fancy the mission," Shackels said. "Says it's too dangerous when there's a proscription going on. He wants your help in finding the bombs quickly."

"Both of us?"

"Yes, both of you."

"That's great!" I cried, rushing out to find Billy Bowden and give him the good news.

We walked up and down the darkened courtyard of the fort. There was nowhere else to be alone except in our cramped quarters.

"What do you think?" said Billy. His face was red with excitement, but he didn't want to be the first to speak out. His technique in our relationship was to ask the questions and get me to do the enthusing. He liked to be the cool one who made the throwaway comment.

"It's exactly what we need," I said, "to complete our frontier experience." We often talked with naive pomposity of our 'experience.' We tended to view life as a series of credits which we earned by doing adventurous things.

"The Tochis know their job," I added.

"By Christ!" Billy spat it out, trying to suppress a delighted grin and observing me out of the corners of his eyes. We both worshipped the Scouts.

A Valentia of 31 Squadron being serviced at Miramshah.

"There's no road through that valley, though," I said. "We'll probably have to run with the *gasht*."

"The hell with that!" Billy hated exercise with a passion and viewed my compulsive tennis and squash playing with disgust. I could see myself running alongside Loppy, mile after mile in the dark, the turbanned Tochis jingling behind us.

Lerwill spoke to us both at dinner and vetoed my dream of trotting through the Madda Khel with the Scouts.

"You'd never be able to keep up with us," he said. "You'd die halfway. I've ordered camels for you from the village."

The next day a villainous looking Pathan, suffering from some affliction of the eyes, led us out of the fort and on to a path beside the river. It would have been a pleasant ride on a horse, but a camel has a nasty lurching gait and it was all we could do to keep ourselves from falling out of the rough saddles. When we rode back into the fort all the officers had assembled to watch us, many of them with cameras. We were wearing turbans, borrowed Tochi shirts and our own khaki trousers. The idea was to be as inconspicuous as possible, but our reception would have been appropriate for a couple of film stars.

The day before our planned expedition the Maharajah of Jodhpur, a prince of fabulous lineage and wealth who was an honorary air commodore in the Indian Air Force, made his official visit to Miramshah. He arrived in his own aeroplane, a bright metal monoplane called a Lockheed Electra, which made our old biplanes look like something out of a history book. It was a great occasion for the fort, and our Wapitis were lined up with pilots and ground crews standing to attention in front of them. The Tochis were resplendant in turbans and baggy trousers and formed a guard of honour. In the afternoon there was a fly-past and all detachment aircraft were airborne, plus a cigar-shaped bomber transport—a Vickers Valentia biplane from 31 Squadron, which had flown in for the event. At night there was a dinner with the Maharajah as honoured guest.

He was a tubby, friendly man. During the day he had worn air force blue uniform with a turban of the same colour. For the evening he wore Indian dress—the equivalent, I suppose, of a Western dinner jacket—a long elaborately embroidered coat and closely fitting white trousers. While the officers were assembling in the anteroom before dinner he circulated freely, clearly wishing to meet as many people as possible. It was not long before I found myself in a group before him.

"How do you like it here in this remote spot?" he asked," chasing the Faqir and his boys?"

"When the army gets close," someone offered, "he just nips over the border."

"Quite so. It's an intractable problem. Major Cobb has told us all about it." Then he abruptly changed the subject. "Have you heard about those two bloody fools?"

His audience froze into silence. No one answered.

"No, sir," I said.

"Oh, it's a great joke. Even the P.A. is in on it. They've convinced them that they must go into the Madda Khel to explode their bombs that didn't go off. As if anyone is going to care about a bomb on top of a mountain! They've been riding camels!" The Maharajah couldn't contain his laughter. He gave a guffaw before going on. "They've dressed them up as Pathans! Can you imagine?"

He looked around him, smiling broadly. Everyone was quiet.

"Have I said anything wrong?" he asked.

"No, sir," I replied. "I'm one of the bloody fools."

5

A LONG HOT SUMMER
15th March 1939 to 1st August 1939

The shame of having our legs pulled faded rapidly after we returned to Kohat. None of the other fellows referred to our camel episode and I can only assume that they felt guilty at taking advantage of our innocence. Someone presented me with a photograph of the two of us, perched on the beasts and looking very foolish, but I can no longer find it in my collection.

On 15th March 1939, the Germans entered Prague and Hitler took Slovakia under his "benevolent protection." In April, Mussolini invaded Albania. Poland was threatened and the prime minister of Great Britain, Mr Neville Chamberlain, indulged in ineffective shuttle diplomacy. However, Hitler's ravings and the dovelike responses of Britain and France, which we read about in the *Frontier Mail* at breakfast time, hardly made a trace on our consciousness. It was as if a silent movie were being played in a corner of a room in which we were doing something of supreme importance, like making love or fighting a duel. The only thing that mattered to us was to get airborne in our dawn-of-flying machines and to be permitted to cruise over the moonscape of this exotic frontier.

Geoffrey running up a Wapiti at Kohat, 1939.

I loved the Westland Wapiti. When the RAF at home was re-equipping to face the Luftwaffe, there was this primitive craft from a bygone era still taking to the air. It wasn't a machine that could have been used in any serious war. Only in this remote place, facing no air opposition, could such an antique design be of practical use.

Billy and I had been trained on comparatively modern types of aircraft that had brakes. The Wapiti had a tailskid, a heavy triangular shoe which dragged over the surface and slowed the aircraft after landing. They were no longer being manufactured and were in such short supply that our commanding officer, Squadron Leader McKechnie, used to keep the shoes locked up in his office safe. This was to guard against 60 Squadron—our sister squadron at Kohat—hogging all the shoes.

Taxiing without brakes was an unfamiliar struggle. The only way to change direction was to put on full rudder and blip the throttle. If this was not judged perfectly, the inertia of the aircraft would exaggerate the turn. Opposite rudder and more engine power had to be applied to retrieve the situation. This led to a build up of speed. The rookie pilot would throttle back instinctively at this point. With no controlling force the Wapiti would go into a ground loop. There was no dual Wapiti to introduce us gently to this monster. We simply strapped ourselves in and drove off to do our best. There were some pretty funny sights when Billy and Lester Davies and I (Lester had travelled with us from England) performed our first circuits and landings. The senior pilots of both squadrons turned out in force to watch and jeer.

Landing was easy. The Hart variants we were accustomed to flying had sensitive undercarts and bounced if a three-point landing was not made, but the heavier Wapiti settled down well onto the ground. The trouble began when the speed fell off and the machine began to swing to one side or the other. If you did nothing the kite would ground loop. If you overused power the speed would build up again. With practice we learned to fight the rudder, kicking rapidly on the rudder bar to prevent the slightest change in direction, until the aircraft came to a halt

Disaster struck on 26th June, a cloudless day when the temperature soon reached 120 degrees in the shade. Flying began at seven o'clock in the morning and the senior pilots had already completed their details when Billy and I taxied out at noon, a decidedly less privileged time. Metal could not be touched without burning the flesh, and we had to climb gingerly into the big open cockpits.

We took off in formation, eight twenty-pound bombs under our wings, to practice dive bombing on the range. Kohat, looking civilized and secure beneath us, sat under a range of hills which stretched southwest to Miramshah and the Afghan frontier. Even in June the *maidan*, the playing fields of the British garrison, were watered and green. The town shimmered in the heat; white, flat-roofed buildings counterpointed by the golden dome of a mosque. The road to Peshawar ran north, winding up the Kohat Pass and disappearing beneath the nose of the 'Old Lady,' a curious rock feature that resembled the profile of a toothless hag.

After we had dropped our bombs, we joined up again for a formation landing. It had been arranged between us that Billy was to lead and I was to follow him. It was not a good idea. Even in perfect conditions a formation landing requires advanced skills. More experienced pilots would have declined to fly in close formation on a day as hot and bumpy as this one, but we had no such fears. Our inspiration was Harry Broadhurst who, a few years earlier, had led the RAF formation team in a series of aerobatics with their wings tied together! He had been a junior pilot in No. 11 Squadron, flying Wapitis out of nearby Risalpur, and many people in the area remembered his vivid presence.

Only one Wapiti sat on the tarmac when we flew over and the aerodrome had a shut down look. Johnny Darwen was on leave prior to returning to England and a mild, ironical Canadian called 'Logger' Powley was standing in for him. It was against the regulations for junior pilots to land in formation, but we were unlikely to be observed at this hour of the day. I signalled to Billy that I was going to stay close and he grinned back at me.

The crosswind leg went well. Billy made a flat approach and kept on a bit of motor, so that I could keep with him by using the throttle in short bursts. If formation flying is to be successful the lead pilot has to maintain a steady throttle setting, and it has to be kept partially open even after touchdown. If he uses insufficient motor the formating pilot has no power differential to play with.

Billy turned into wind and reduced speed for the landing. The bumps became more violent as we approached the ground. Crossing the airfield boundary, a downdraft yanked us towards the earth. Billy looked at me, something near to panic on his face. It was a fatal glance, for he ceased to concentrate on his own flying. We were both going slowly, not far from the stall and twenty feet from the ground.

Billy's Wapiti suddenly dropped heavily.

I had been concentrating on keeping formation, but by half watching my airspeed I had kept in the glide. By the time I could react to what had happened I was already on the ground and fast overtaking him. He had struck with such an impact that it had almost stopped his progress. His undercarriage was beginning to collapse sideways and he slewed to the left directly in my path. The Wapiti had a way of lurching to the left once the speed began to fall off. As he swung across me I pushed on full left rudder to avoid a crash. To keep straight at this point I needed full right rudder, so it is easy to see that I was encouraging my Wapiti to do what came naturally. It turned away ecstatically, an arrow from the bow, in a sharp tightening arc to the left .

As soon as I was clear of Billy's aircraft I tried to regain control. Since the Wapiti had no brakes, all I could do was to stamp on opposite rudder. Nothing happened. Its parabola had achieved by that point a certain sweeping inevitability. I opened the throttle to give the rudder more bite, but the speed increased

above: Billy Bowden's machine after the crash
with the author's machine in the background.
below: The author's machine.

and the turn tightened. I gave up the idea as hopeless and throttled back. Simultaneously a bowstring snapped with a twanging noise beneath me.

As my speed fell off, the turn miraculously straightened out and I was back where I landed. I had run in a circle and was now sliding towards Billy's stationary Wapiti. Twenty yards short of impact my undercarriage collapsed sideways, the starboard wing slumped to the ground and I came to rest. There we were, close together in the middle of the small grass airfield, a tragic heap of splintered wood and crumpled canvas.

In minutes the previously deserted field was filled with trucks bearing technicians and some jeering pilots from 27 and 60 Squadrons. Everybody loves a crash and this was a double event. Billy and I stood glumly in the midday heat while a technical warrant officer and his staff made notes of damage, measured distances, set out fire extinguishers and performed all the melancholy tasks that accompany a crash. An airman from the photographic section set up a tripod to take official pictures.

> Diary entry: 30th June 1939
> The station adjutant, Slim Olney, was president of the Court of Enquiry. It was held in one of the offices in station headquarters and it took most of the morning. Billy and I sat there while the various technical witnesses made their depositions and were questioned. Billy was very upset, particularly at the long list of damaged parts and parts beyond repair on his aircraft. His face was scarlet the whole time. Mind you, his kite was WRECKED. Mine was slightly the worse for wear.
> When questioned by Olney, Billy had no defence. He just admitted that he'd PRANGED! Slim turned to me and said, "What is your explanation?" I told him I made a good landing and then something went wrong that was beyond my control. "You weren't distracted by Bowden's crash?" "No," I said. "Something twanged and broke underneath me. I heard it distinctly. Then

I lost control. It was impossible to keep the aircraft running in a straight line."

Slim did not seem convinced. However, almost the last witness was Sergeant Cundall, the 'C' Flight rigger, and he said the locknuts on the undercarriage crossbracing wires were incorrectly adjusted, causing one of the wires to break loose and eventually collapsing the undercart. 1 was at once exonerated from blame. Billy, however, was convicted of "Gross Carelessness" and a note to that effect was put in his log book, signed by the station commander.

After it was all over, Olney was very nice to Billy. He told him not to take it too hard. But Billy is taking it hard. I can't get a smile out of him. The strange thing is that no mention was made of the fact that we were landing in formation without authorization. Perhaps Slim Olney wanted to let us off that one.

The temperature stuck at 120 degrees in the shade for three weeks and the station medical officer, a sweaty man who looked out of place on the North West Frontier, went mad. He began walking about the mess garden at night in feminine underwear and was whisked away to a sanatorium in the hills. Those who could get away on leave went to Murree, the local hill station, where the air was cool and the wives and daughters of the military offered prospects of recreation.

I engaged a *munshi* to give me Urdu lessons. He was an elderly Pathan with a dignified bearing, always dressed in a white business suit with an expensive *pagri* on his head. I started out with high hopes but soon became faint-hearted at the prospect of what I had to learn; not only a new language but a new script. I wasted time asking about Persian poetry. He quoted me a verse of Hafiz. "When the bee settles on the flower, the moth dies vainly." It is a riddle. The bee collects honey from the flower and deposits it in wax cells. Men gather the honey and make candles with the wax. The candle is lit and the moth, attracted by the flame, burns its wings and dies. The poetry is in a different tradition and does not translate well. The pleasure is partly in the diction and partly in solving the riddle.

One evening we were discussing the inevitable British withdrawal from India and the propaganda emanating from the Indian National Congress to hurry up the process.

"Sir," he said, wagging his head wisely, "the Hindus will end up having their throats cut."

"Why, Munshi?"

"We Musselmans will march to the south and take our country again. We have ruled India for a thousand years. We will not be dictated by them. They are a filthy people."

He was obviously expecting my approval. He had said similar things to other officers learning Urdu and they had laughed and smiled. The British in India seemed to favour Muslims, perhaps because Mahatma Gandhi's independence movement was overwhelmingly Hindu. The only Hindus I knew were Shackels Majumdar and the Maharajah of Jodhpur, but I didn't see why humbler members of that religion deserved to have their throats cut. We parted coldly and I sent my bearer, Selim Khan, to pay him for his time and to cancel further lessons.

The airfield at Kohat was two miles south of the town and some distance from the officers' mess, which was in the cantonment. This had some advantages. Early morning testing of aero engines was distant to the ear. Night flying was less intrusive. Conversation at the dinner table did not have to cease while take-offs were in progress. Walking outside in the evening one would see the twinkling lights of the circling Wapitis and hear very little noise. The main disadvantage was that we couldn't walk to work from the mess, as we could always do on a self-enclosed station. A canvas-topped military truck, with wooden benches screwed to each wall, would pick us up at 7.30 am to take us to the flights. Officers would pile in and sit down, displaying two

above: Street scene in Kohat.
below: Cavalry parading at Kohat, 1939.

rows of brown knees sticking out of freshly ironed khaki shorts. The vehicle looked crammed with knees and tropical topis, all khaki coloured. At one o'clock the same truck would return us to the mess for lunch. Knees and topis looked the same, but the starch had gone out of the shorts.

It was wisdom to sleep in the afternoons as the Indians did. After a glass of cold Murree beer and a good meal we would stretch out on our beds under a whirling electric fan and be asleep in a moment. Sleep in the afternoon was called 'charp time' *charpoy* being the Urdu word for bed. In the evening the temperature would drop a bit. There was a swimming pool in the mess garden, ringed with a high hedge to preserve our nakedness from the Pathans, who would have disapproved. Mess servants, resplendant in their quasi-military uniforms, would bring ice cold beer and hot sausages. We seemed to be perpetually hungry. After dinner an airman would erect a screen on the lawn and a film would be shown.

All the officers messes were set in a ring around the playing fields of the maidan. The Kohat Officers Club, which sat on a low hill to the north, dominated the scene. It was a fine white building in the style of Lutyens' New Delhi, with a pillared portico and a flight of six steps. Walking across for library books I'd see the cavalry regiment playing polo. In hot weather they saved their mounts by playing slow chukkers, polo in slow motion. It was an elegant sight and there was usually a gathering of Indians and Europeans to watch. There were a lot of jokes about the cavalry, partly because they were perceived to put on airs and partly because they benefitted from government funded polo, since their games were theoretically parades. Their officers were lean and horsey and had drawls that went beyond the usual limits. The joke was that horse cavalry was already a thing of the past. Within a few years they would all be wearing humble berets and driving tanks. However they made up for their air of superiority by being the provider of horses to the garrison. In order to function as a military unit they needed to have many more horses on hand than they could exercise. Any officer who applied would be loaned a fine horse and the fodder to feed it. The snag was that you had to pay for your own groom (*syce*), though the monthly pay of a groom was not much. I remember with some shame that I paid a retired NCO from a cavalry regiment fifteen rupees a month to look after my mount. He lived over the stable with his wife and four children. Every day at 5.30 am he would bring the horse to my door and I would ride out into the country for an hour.

The town was only a few streets away and I'd wander through the bazaar in the evening, wishing that I had the gift of tongues and could communicate with these strangers; wishing that I'd not quarrelled with the *munshi* and had persisted with my study. It puzzled me to see young Pathans of warlike appearance hand in hand like lovers. But this may be a Western interpretation. I once saw Selim Khan swinging the hand of another young bearer, quite unembarrassed. He salaamed me politely but did not release his hold on his companion. The women were a total mystery, enveloped in shapeless garments and heavily veiled. I was always disappointed that the fall of a garment from the head, with its little observation grille, did not so much as hint at the female shape beneath.

Hot weather seems to breed crazy behaviour. Aircraftsman Brougham, a fitter in 'C' Flight, had been charged with some minor offence. He was a surly fellow with a sound reputation as an engineer. He would not accept the punishment of a few days confined to barracks and was remanded to the C.O. In the station commander's office he behaved with open truculence and demanded a court martial. He was sentenced to twenty-one days detention for insubordination and was marched off shouting and cursing. There was no RAF detention centre in such a remote place as Kohat, so he was transferred to the civilian prison.

As I see it now, trying to understand how such a thing could have occurred, he must have been ill with heat exhaustion and should have been hospitalized rather than punished. The local gaol was an abomination. His cell was small and dirty. In the furious heat of that June there were no fans to modify the torture. He was the only European in the prison and must have felt himself abandoned by the world. On the third night he hanged himself.

Summer was the suicide season in India. Officers who had sweated in the plains all June and July would take leave to visit their families in the hill stations. Some would find their wives involved with other men. I never heard of any murders, strangely enough. It always seemed to be the chivalrous husband who voluntarily removed himself from the scene. This extreme reaction to commonplace domestic tragedy was typical of British life in India. It was caused in part by the heat and the necessary separation of families; and in part by the chronic scarcity of women and the corresponding inflation of their value.

Men in barracks were worse off than the officers, who had comfortable clubs to go to and in the cool months a minimal contact with the wives and daughters of other officers. The airmen's barracks were gloomy and devoid of beauty. I would sometimes carry out 'C' Flight kit inspections, and they looked to me like cattle sheds. On either side of the long, high ceilinged wooden hut fifty beds were arranged at exact intervals. Punkahs, or fans, swung heavily overhead. They consisted of oblong sheets of stiff canvas, attached to an iron framework that moved noisily back and forth, stirring up the stagnant air. An Indian, *punkah wallah*, kept the contraption in motion by pulling rhythmically on a rope with his foot. Sometimes at night, or in the middle of a hot afternoon, the operator would get drowsy and the fan would come to rest. Then the sleeping airmen would wake up in pools of sweat and scream at him to get going again.

Sometime in the 19th century brothels for troops were outlawed. This had the effect of making a grim and lonely life closer to intolerable. It was still possible to find a prostitute in the back streets of Kohat, but without government inspection there was a

above: The author as Duty Pilot, Kohat, 1939.
below: Billy Bowden, 'Bowden Sahib,' at Kohat Mess.

virtual certainty of acquiring a disease. Only in large towns, like Lahore or Karachi, which had a population of Anglo-Indians to welcome him to their clubs and homes, did the average airman have any opportunity for social life. Nothing much had changed since Kipling's time, and a single man in barracks was still one of the forgotten men.

By July we had acquired sufficient service to be eligible for leave. Officers who had gone before us came back talking of cool weather, parties until dawn and conquests over women. I was ready for some civilized recreation but Billy scorned the flesh-pots. He came to my room one evening after charp time with his face set and determined. We sat in deck chairs on the verandah of our quarters overlooking the shadowed tennis courts. The sun was down but the day's heat had barely moderated. I longed to be cool and at the same time itched to play tennis, but my chest was covered with prickly heat rash and the doctor had warned me off hard exercise. Selim Khan brought in tea and toast. It strikes me now that a bearer had a long day. It started at 6 am and ended about 7 pm when his sahib, having bathed, could be depatched, properly clothed for the evening, towards dinner at the mess.

"Murree sounds a grand place," I said, kicking it off.

"Poodle-faking!" Billy spat out the words. It was the current euphemism for chasing women and had a contemptuous ring to it.

"What's wrong with that? I haven't seen a girl since we leapt off the boat. I'm starved for love and affection."

"But it's a waste of bloody time, man. Flocks of subalterns chasing one ugly female. Forget it!"

Billy was pumped up, his grin a blend of fierceness and embarrassment at his own animation. I saw his point about the flocks of subalterns.

"You never know your luck," I said, weakening a little.

"If you go to Murree it will be just like being back on the *Neuralia*. It's another boat deck half way up a perishing mountain. You'll get a stingy kiss for your trouble and it won't be worth the time you spent to earn it. You don't want to go through that Desiree Tyrrell business again."

"I liked that girl," I said, recalling the thrill of those embraces. Such a precious few before she pulled me down the companionway to the safety of the crowded lounge.

"There isn't time for girls. We've got two weeks. We can go on a trek."

"A trek?"

"Kashmir. I've been looking at it on the map. It's bang up against China. We can hire mules and trek as far as we can up one of the valleys. He fished a map from the pocket of his dressing gown. "Look! The Kolohoi glacier. It's within striking distance of Srinagar."

6

THE HIGH HIMALAYAS
1st August 1939 to 23rd August 1939

We boarded a slow uncomfortable train to Jammu and travelled by bus to Srinagar. We were the only Europeans in a vehicle crowded with Indians. Half the passengers were children. Furniture and bedding and boxes of live chickens were strapped to the roof, making it look topheavy. The road wound upward interminably and the bus creaked in the turns. As it leaned out over the precipices its load shifted audibly. Whole families seemed to be moving to a new location with all their worldly goods. Most of them were Muslims, their women swathed in white garments, but not totally veiled as they would have been in the Frontier Province. Faces and hands showed, but little else. A Hindu family, the young wife looking conspicuously attractive in a colourful sari, sat quietly at the back. After an hour the way steepened and the noise of the overtaxed engine dominated the children's chatter. Two stops had to be made for the engine to cool down, and all the passengers dismounted and stood at a distance from the bus as if it might go off like a bomb. As we approached Srinagar we could see torrents flowing through gorges and frail rope bridges swaying above them. Massive peaks in the background looked like a stage set.

above: A lake scene at Srinagar.
below: The rugged beauty of the Himalayas.

Srinagar is a city of canals, like Venice, built out on stilts over the broad Jhelum River. The wooden houses lean over the water, piled on top of one another. Houseboats, swarming with Kashmiri life, were moored in the sidestreams and backwaters. We had been told it was a centre for prostitution but Billy and I were in no mood to repeat our Port Said experience. We spent one night in a hotel and moved into a rented houseboat on the Nagim Bagh, a lake filled with water lilies just outside the city. Servants and a cook were provided in the package. Clustered about us were other houseboats, rented by military people and their families. We looked over the lake at the Himalayan range, with the white peak of Nanga Parbat dominating. A single motor boat was dragging a water skier and it seemed like a profanation.

The day after we arrived I met a girl. She came running down the path towards me as I was setting out to buy provisions. She stopped when she saw me and we laughed and introduced ourselves. She told me that her name was Penelope Fortescue and that her father was a major on the staff at GHQ, Delhi. They were on their last week of a month-long holiday. She accepted my invitation to visit the Shalimar gardens, which I'd been told was a two-hour boat ride across the lake. Billy was disgusted.

"What about the trek?" he protested."We have a whole day's work to organize it. I need you for the planning. There's no time to waste on rot like girls."

"This comes first," I replied. "You can die a bachelor if you like."

I was ludicrously handicapped for romance and part of me feared it. The boy's school I had attended, run by Benedictine monks, had given me the notion that better spirits went into the church. I was a dropout from that scheme but had not embraced any other. The convent girls in their dark blue gymslips who were marched by nuns into our Tuesday afternoon Benediction services were the only figures of glamour for our imaginations to grip on. Their skirts were short, to permit athletic activities like netball, and they wore black stockings and low-heeled black shoes. This garb must have seemed sensible and modest to the nuns, but generations of boys could not have conceived a sexier costume. However, we had no means of making contact with these goddesses. Beyond the boatdeck episode I had no sexual experience, and I was over excited in the presence of young females, particularly if they were attractive.

I hired a punt from a small flotilla of them at a nearby dock. The boatmen were so eager to be hired that in order to choose it was necessary to quell a mob first. She was waiting for me on the deck of her father's houseboat wearing a dress of white silk which blew against her in the breeze. I noticed white sandals and a white handbag which she held in both hands as if she feared to drop it. She was really beautiful in a blonde Grace Kelly sort of style. I stood up to hand her down into the boat and we settled on the long bench seat, which was well supplied with cushions. The boatman was a stocky boy who dressed with surprising formality in a gold skullcap, a richly embroidered waistcoat and baggy trousers. He stood at the rear of his heavy punt and poled us across the interlinked waters, steering between islands of blooming lotuses.

I desperately wanted to impress this girl, but except for a bit of dancing and horsing around on the *SS Neuralia* I had no experience of talking to girls. We were alone (the boatman knew no English) and nothing was going on except the flower-filled lake and the majestic background of the Himalayas. I was twenty years of age, hale and hearty, and celibate as few could imagine today. I was fit to bust. If I did not speak I would fall at her feet and clasp her knees and be carted off to hospital like the unfortunate medical officer at Kohat.

"Do you know anything about the Shalimar gardens?" I asked.

"No, I ..."

"Well, the Mogul emperors loved to get away from the heat of the plains—just like we do—and so they built summer palaces in the foothills. Akbar conquered all this part of the world in the

16th century, but it was probably his son, Jahangir, or his grandson, Shah Jehan, in the 17th, who built the gardens up here."

She did not reply. I had obviously bombed. In my confusion I had begun talking in the manner of my elder brother Ken, who was always precise about dates and names and historical events. He would go on for hours describing Hannibal's victory at Lake Trasimene or the tactics of Fabius Cunctator. The library at the Kohat club was crammed with books about India, and I had been reading them steadily since my arrival. But all this information was of no use for flirtatious talk between the sexes. I was only practiced in two subjects, though—literature and flying—both equally fatal. In my misery and desperation I tried to be funny.

"Do you know the song, 'Pale Hands I Love Beside the Shalimar'?"

"I don't think so."

"My father would sing it on Sunday afternoons," I said. "My mother played the piano accompaniment. It was very moving."

I then sang a verse of "Pale Hands" in my father's fruity baritone voice. At home the family would go into fits of laughter at this rendition. I was accustomed to having it well received.

Penelope pursed her lips and froze.

To this day I cannot fathom exactly what my offence was. It could have been the middle class scene I had painted of our household. The sing song after Sunday dinner. The Dickensian sentimentality. Her name was Fortescue. Did her social rank preclude such things?

The silence—which she did not violate—was too much for me. I stuck it out for ten long minutes, but I could bear no more. I elaborated on the Mogul conquest of India. I told her that Shah Jehan had built the Taj Mahal for his dead wife. I related how General John Nicholson was killed by the walls of the Red Fort in Delhi during the Indian Mutiny. I murdered my chances with ruthless efficiency, knowing that I was doing so, unable to control my mouth.

above: A houseboat at Nagim Bagh, Kashmir.
below: The Shalimar Gardens, Nagim Bagh, Kashmir.

I had dreamed of falling in love with—and being loved by—
a beautiful girl such as this. The natural splendour of the mountain scenery, the dramatic contrast between the field of flowers on
the quiet lake and the soaring peaks, made my failure all the more
painful. It would have been glorious if she had responded to me,
but it was my fault she hadn't. I was a nerd. And how was I to
learn anything of love if my performance grew worse in propor-
tion to the attractions of the lady? I was a hopeless case.

The Shalimar gardens were admirably restrained. In Europe
such a garden would be filled with gesticulating statues and
important buildings, but the Islamic style had produced here a
low key structure that did not challenge the Himalayas. It was
deliberately tactful. Penelope and I walked around and shared a
sandwich lunch sitting on a stone wall; but by this time conversation had lapsed completely. We hardly exchanged a word as the
boatman pushed us back through the idyllic landscape.

"Thank you for a very nice day," she said, shaking my hand
and quickly crossing the wooden catwalk to the safety of her
father's boat. She'd marry, I thought bitterly, some stupid subaltern and live on the Salisbury Plain. I would die a bachelor.

When I told Billy the story of my humiliation, he had no
comment beyond an expression of exaggerated contempt. He
launched at once into the details of our expedition. He had
arranged with a contractor to provide a guide, three mules and a
gun bearer. We were to take a shotgun, a light rifle and a heavy
calibre rifle capable of killing a bear.,

"I'm not interested in shooting big game," I said.

"Neither am I," he replied. "I just couldn't put him off.
According to his ideas, two sahibs going off into the wilderness
must be after game. I didn't know how to convey to him that it
was the journey itself that we were interested in."

At six o'clock the next morning we set out on foot, led by
our guide, a thin middle-aged Muslim who had a reassuring air of

Kashmiri women and children in Kashmir.

command. The Kolohoi Valley reminded me of Chinese drawings in which the mountains were impossibly vast, the landscape hardly containable within the frame, and the human element dwarfed by the gigantic folds and forests. We walked ahead of the mules through this oversized paradise, reminding ourselves in as many ways as we could tell, that we were really there, that we were farther into the heart of Asia than Samarkand. We felt that we were making our way over the back of the world and that Shangri La was only a few miles further on up a mountain track.

As we passed by the hill villages the inhabitants turned out to watch us. The men were short and thick, with muscular legs. The women were unveiled and wore bright-coloured layered skirts, showing full figures through their embroidered tunics. They held their children up to wave at us. In the open country we came across twenty young monks in saffron robes who smiled and spoke incomprehensible blessings before disappearing uphill.

After three days of climbing steadily to the east we reached an altitude of eleven thousand feet. The floor of the valley had become quite narrow, less than a mile across, and the canted slabs of the mountains were heaped around us. We camped near a corn-field, just outside a small village. The mules had been unloaded and the tents were going up. We had submitted to the good advice of the contractor to employ a cook, and he was already busy starting a fire for the evening meal. Billy and I sat on a boulder smoking, our round tins of Craven 'A' cork-tipped cigarettes beside us, watching the bustle with some satisfaction. We felt fit and tired after our long uphill walk.

There was still some light in the sky, but the valley was dark. The guide had hung an oil lamp at the entrance to our tent and was setting out a table and two canvas chairs. We were far away from the heat of Kohat and the scenes of our errors and humiliations. Billy was chalking up credits in some imaginery account book, weighing our adventure against those failures. He mentioned

Peter Fleming,[1] who was one of our heroes. We'd have loved to have pressed on through the high passes to Tartary.

"I wonder how far we can go?" said Billy.

"To the world's rim," I replied, making an extravagant gesture, my cigarette glowing like a comet in the dark.

While we were eating chicken curry and washing it down with Murree beer, the village headman approached accompanied by some other elders. They engaged in a long conversation with our guide. Finally they all came towards us and salaamed. The guide interpreted.

"The headman says, sir, that a bear comes from the mountain and eats corn. He is asking sahib to shoot the bear."

"Are there no guns in the village?"

"No, sir. There is no gun." I looked at Billy in amazement. His face was beginning to flush at the prospect of a bear shoot, and he put his thumbs up. It had become our responsibility to shoot a bear. The contractor's insistence on our travelling with a powerful rifle was beginning to make sense.

"Where does it live," I asked.

"Too far up the mountain, sir. It will come to eat tonight. We will wait in the cornfield and shoot it."

Easier said than done. The cornfield ran from the south side of the village to the lowest reaches of the valley where a torrent roared. Beyond was a forested hillside and beyond that a vast, bare mountain. It was a dead black night and we had not thought to buy a flashlight in Srinagar. No one in the village had any means of illumination beyond oil lamps, which would scare the animal off. We were travelling with one heavy and one light rifle, and it was agreed that I would take the heavy one. But it wasn't clear to either of us how a bear could be killed under circumstances of

---

[1] Peter Fleming , the author of *Brazilian Adventure* and *News From Tartary*, was at the time more famous than his younger brother, Ian Fleming, author of the James Bond books.

total darkness. Excitement in the village, though, was palpable. Miracles were anticipated when Englishmen with their mules and weaponry came on the scene.

We slept till three in the morning and were awakened by the gun bearer. Minutes later we were settled in the middle of a field halfway down the slope. There was a loud sound of rushing water. About fifty villagers came with us and sat silently on the ground in the darkness as an hour went by. Then we heard the bear crashing through the forest. Without pausing to sniff out an ambush, he moved noisily into the field and at once began eating. As he ate, he moved towards us. For twenty minutes we listened to his crunching and heavy breathing as he got closer and closer. Finally we could smell him. I saw a dark shape against the stars and the gun bearer whispered, "Shoot, sahib." Billy and I both let fly at the same moment. The report of the rifles was deafening and I'd forgotten in my excitement to jam the butt firmly to my shoulder. The recoil thumped me backwards. In the flash of the explosions I caught the movement of a large form in rapid retreat, downslope and to the left. Then we heard the blundering noises, the crashing of a heavy body through twigs and branches, as the bear made its way up the hillside. It was clearly uninjured.

We went to bed rather disconsolate, and woke late. The head-man was waiting for us, sitting crosslegged at the opening to our tent talking to the guide. They pointed eagerly upwards. Above the tree line the bear was visible, a brown smudge on the stony expanse of the mountain. When we stepped out of the tent the whole village thronged around us. We sat at our folding table eating breakfast while the older people stared at us gravely and the youngsters danced and played and pointed excitedly at the bear.

"All the people will chase the bear now," explained the guide. "They will drive the bear down and you will shoot."

We set out within the hour and, as the guide had forecast, all the inhabitants, except mothers with children in arms, turned out for the hunt. The men walked alongside us, talking animatedly. Little boys and some girls in pretty costumes, ran ahead. The older youths led the party, armed with staves.

From the valley the bare expanse of hillside stretched like a tilted sea. A mile above us was the bear, apparently sleeping but clearly recognizeable in the morning sunshine. From ten o'clock until two in the afternoon we toiled uphill. The bear snoozed on, ignoring this organized invasion of his wilderness. The older boys had by this time climbed high up the slope and were closing in above him. It was a colourful sight. A procession of brown youngsters, the boys wearing gold skull caps that flashed in the sunlight, were scampering to complete a ring which would cut off the bear's escape.

Just as the human noose was closing, he roused himself and looked round. He shook his hide like a dog shaking water off his coat after a swim. He paused for a second and then made off directly up the mountain, aiming for the narrowing gap. His progress was so swift that there was no chance of blocking his escape. With a few powerful strides he shot upwards, easily evading the men whose shouts we could hear. In a few seconds he had disappeared into the landscape as if into a cloud.

Billy and I, our guns cocked, stared at one another in dismay. Billy was flushing as he always did when embarrassed. We were both thinking the same thing. We'd done it again! It was another Port Said, another spoof camel ride into the Madda Khel, another double crash with spectators. And a whole village this time to join in the jeering. But these people (who I bless in retrospect) took a different view of unsuccess. Shrieks of joy and shouts of laughter were heard from the leading beaters. The little children near me danced and sang and the adults waved their arms in the air. Everyone smiled on us and thanked us. There was no expression of disappointment or rage at all. It could have been sympathy for us or sheer good manners. It surely must have been a serious issue that would send an entire population out on to a mountainside for a day that could be more usefully employed. But perhaps they had enjoyed the outing. Remotely situated in the wildest country and almost a week's march from the nearest town, they might have been grateful for the entertainment.

"You know what I think," Billy said, late that night as we turned over the events of the day. "Fifty years from now they'll be telling their grandchildren how two stupid Englishmen couldn't kill a bear that was right in front of their eyes."

The next day we climbed for most of the daylight hours and camped below the glacier. It was chilly at 15,000 feet. I've seen glaciers from the air since then, flowing like candle grease down the Greenland fiords to the open sea. They must be one of nature's grandest spectacles, breaking into glassy iceburgs and drifting off to endanger shipping. Walking on one was a disappointment. We spent a dogged day clambering over its uneven and dangerous surface. It was just a river of ice, mixed with boulders large and small, moving with imperceptible slowness down the back of a mountain.

"That," I said, as we huddled in our tent that evening, "was a glacier."

"Bloody bore," he grumbled.

The expedition had been inexpensive. After paying the contractor and tipping the guide and his men, we still had plenty of cash when we arrived back in Kohat. The cheapness of goods and services was an aspect of life in India that amazed us. All the British military were paid at a higher rate than those at home, and even pilot officers in the RAF lived in a somewhat princely fashion. I shared a bungalow with a brother officer and we each had a separate sitting room, bedroom, lavatory and bathroom. Every room was equipped with an electric fan suspended from a high ceiling. Even the furniture was designed in the grand manner. I had two large leather club chairs, a desk, a long centre table and a settee, and there was plenty of space to walk around.

above: The author and gunbearer in the Kolohoi Valley.
below: Our campsite in the Kolohoi Valley.

Five servants were required to keep a British officer from doing anything for himself. The choice of a bearer was critical, because he was the intermediary between the ignorant Britisher and the strangely formal world of Indian servants. When Billy and I arrived with all our luggage at the portico of the Kohat officers mess in November 1938, there were at least twenty bearers waiting to be hired by the new sahibs. Their ages ranged from grizzled men in their sixties to beardless youths. We had two brass-bound chests and several suitcases each, and it was clear that this mound of luggage near the mess steps could not be moved until we chose our bearers. There was much shouting and jostling. Written recommendations from long-gone sahibs were waved in the air. Billy was taken by an old man who spoke good English and who explained that he would be the perfect choice for a young gentleman. I showed little resistance when a handsome Pathan in official RAF mess uniform gained my attention by flashing a blue eyed smile and saying, "I am Flight Lieutenant Lambert's bearer, sir. This is my brother, Selim Khan. I have taught him everything, sir. He will serve you well, sir." Selim was tall like his brother and also had blue eyes. But he was a mere stripling of seventeen years. I hesitated, and my hesitation was taken as assent. Lambert's bearer issued some orders in imperious Pashtu and my luggage disappeared as rapidly as the crowd of disappointed applicants.

I learned afterwards that Selim Khan was a *chokra,* the word for a young man who has not won his spurs, and all the other bearers were of superior rank to him. This caused me to be served last at the dining table; but I was told that his formidable brother often came to his rescue. However strange it may seem, blue eyes are not uncommon on the Northwest Frontier. Could it be European blood brought in by the Macedonian infantry of Alexander the Great? Or is it more recent than that? Perhaps the ill-paid soldiers of the Queen so badly trashed under General Elphinstone? Afghan women are said to be partial to fairskinned children.

Other servants had to be employed the same day; a gardener (*mali*), a sweeper (*mehtar*) and a night watchman (*chowkidar*). Later a groom for my cavalry horse (*syce*) was added. The chowkidar was a necessity. His trade was linked to the class of thieves. If you employed a chowkidar, even if he smoked hashish (*bhang*) on your front porch until he was glassy eyed, and then slept all night without stirring, you would never be robbed. If you chose not to employ him, you certainly would. In the lavatory was a commode, referred to as a 'thunder box' which was emptied by the sweeper, a person of the Hindu 'untouchable' class. Immediately you vacated the lavatory the sweeper entered by the outside door—no sweeper ever entered the house proper—and removed the waste. It was one of those aspects of Indian life that were at once funny and pathetic. Did he stay all day outside the door waiting for a deposit? Why was only one group of dark skinned outcasts permitted to do this job? Why did they remain outcasts, when they could embrace Islam and rid themselves of the stigma forever? If encountered sweeping the paths, they would paper themselves against the walls of the mess in exaggerated humility.

The absence of running water was a bit strange, but the disadvantage was modified by servant-power. Hot water was available at any time simply by asking for it. The bearer would rush off to some hidden source and hurry back to fill the wash basin. The evening bath was quite an event, with the bearer supervising servants of lower status who brought in what looked like oversized soup tureens, filled with boiling water. They were made of galvanized iron and had metal covers to preserve heat. The operation required at least three men, two to lift the tureen by its handles and a bearer to organize the affair and finally to bring in a kettle of cold water to get the temperature just right. Then, when all was prepared, the sahib would be called to his bath, handed the soap, and the bearer would stand by with towels. I suppose this procedure, with its orderly bustle, would have been familiar to the aristocracy and gentry of England right up to modern times. In great houses, like Blenheim Palace, where the kitchens are distant from the living rooms, one may presume that the hot water cooled considerably by the time it reached the tub.

By the weird Victorian standards that were still in vogue, officers weren't expected to marry before the age of thirty. If they did it was considered a black mark and harmful to their careers. They were denied marriage allowance and couldn't live in the comfortable quarters provided for those who played the game correctly. 'Bum' Thomas, a young flying officer in 27 Squadron, was married and lived with his wife in sub-standard quarters in the town. He was a pleasant fellow with large buttocks that were seen to advantage in khaki shorts. The sad thing was that he was virtually ostracised because of his marital status and his lack of money. We hardly saw him at all off duty, and he departed sheepishly after dinner on guest nights, before the real drinking began. Nearly all the marrieds were senior people. Their staffs included a professional cook (*khansamah*) who lived on the premises in accomodation suited to his high position among the household servants. In a remote station, with no entertainment outside the little community of Europeans, food was a burning issue. A good khansamah was a prized possession and there was always the danger that he would be lured away by some other officer for higher wages. But servants could be abominably treated. One of our squadron leaders had an uneasy relationship with his wife, who was a fierce and demanding woman. Whenever they quarrelled he would retaliate by losing his appetite and picking at his food, a tactic that enraged her. Her revenge on him was to sack the khansamah. She ran through several of them a year.

If the couple had young children there would have to be a nanny (*ayah*). The British wife, called 'memsahib' by her servants, had little work to do beyond giving orders for the proper regulation of the household and entertaining for her husband. Servants, however, did need watching. One of our wives was puzzled by the way her baby, an active child of twelve months, would go instantly to sleep as soon as the ayah put her down. Watching one day, she saw the ayah take a thumb from the child's mouth and smear something on the nail. "What is that?" she asked. "A little bit of opium, memsahib," was the reply. The ayah was dismissed at once.

In another household the bearer beat his wife. He was a young goodlooking Pathan and had married an ugly widow for her money. When he strayed from the path of virtue, she remonstrated with him and he thrashed her. She then ran to the memsahib, who told her husband, and the bearer was threatened with dismissal. But it happened again and again. These were the dramas that one heard of at dinner parties in the cantonment. There was an irony in these middle-class British people talking of their servants in somewhat the same humorous and condescending vein as the dukes and duchesses of Trollope or the Anglo-Irish gentry of *Reminiscences of an Irish R.M.*

There was a rigid system by which the unmarried officers were introduced to the married community. As soon as a new officer arrived on a station he was told to drop cards on the commanding officer, his wife, and all other married officers. Billy and I had solemnly walked out one afternoon and dropped ours in the boxes provided. It didn't involve meeting any of them. The bungalows were set back in ample grounds and the wooden boxes were attached to the whitewashed brick gateposts on the road. In due course we were invited to cocktail parties. We also called on the army, but only on their senior officers, the brigadier and the colonels of regiments. The result was that we met a cross section of our fellows at Kohat quite quickly. In a single party one could meet, and have some kind of converse with, a captain in the cavalry, a squadron leader's wife, a subaltern in the army signals just out from England, and the young handsome second wife of the brigade major.

*   *   *

I finally got used to the antics of my cavalry horse, a fiery steed which had the bad habit of rearing on its hind legs before allowing me to mount it. The regiment always had troops under training and I attended their morning sessions, crossed my stirrups and jogged with the rest of them. When the time came for jumping, the major in charge did not relax his ban on the use of stirrups and to my surprise I learnt to jump without them.

The worst aspect of my life was the restriction on flying. Because of the tense political situation in Europe the use of aviation fuel was rationed by government order. Pilots were only allowed to fly a maximum of twelve hours a month, a figure designed to keep experienced people in practice, but ignoring the needs of rookies like ourselves who were just out of basic training. Luckily there was trouble on the frontier and we continued to drop bombs on the grazing areas of the Ahmadzai, which involved intoxicating low flying over wild terrain. But there was never enough flying. We hung around the flight commander's office in the hope of picking up an air test and were shooed away to sort maps in the navigation section. During the long hours between flights and in the empty hours of stifling heat each evening as we sat with towels round our waists under the overhead fans, we comforted ourselves by planning the next trek. My dream—which would have been realized if Hitler had not started a war—was to rendezvous with my brother in Samarkand.

Ken was three years older and for most of my early life he had ignored me in favour of his own friends. I yearned to be part of their games but was only allowed to join them for swimming. I soon became an expert swimmer, but the experience of being drowned by older boys is still with me as a recurrent dream. Ken discovered me when I was thirteen and changed my life. In the family I was known affectionally as 'the egg,' because my mind was always elsewhere.

above: The ancient car owned by Billy Bowden and the author on the road to Peshawar.   *below*: The winding road through the storied Khyber Pass.

Ken found where my mind was when he was struggling to remember some lines of Shakespeare and I quoted the whole speech by heart. In our oversize Victorian lavatory at home there was a shelf of books. Shakespeare's *Sonnets* and Boswell's *Life of Dr. Samuel Johnson* were always there. Other books of similar status were added from time to time. I absorbed and unconsciously memorized this material, absenting myself from the everyday world and doing very badly at school, except in English and history. Ken was interested in the same subjects, but his intelligence was different from mine, more comprehensive and efficient. "You can't fail the School Certificate," he once told me. "That would be absurd." And I rushed off to study Mathematics and French so as not to earn his disrespect.

Quite soon he dropped all his friends and we became inseparable, spending our holidays walking through Germany, Ireland and the Lake District. Ken read voraciously in history, literature and philosophy, and I read everything that he read. It was his idea to work at boring but well-paid jobs until we had enough money to sustain a magnificent adventure—a walk that might take years, through Europe and across the back of Asia to China. After that we would settle down, get married and have families.

Ken had joined the investment department of Schroders Bank in the City of London as one of their up-and-coming "young men," and had been saving money while I was still at school. My motive for taking a short service commission in the Royal Air Force was to match his funds by earning the gratuity of four hundred pounds at the end of four years. However, as soon as I began to fly aeroplanes—getting an unfair advantage over him in the realm of adventure—Ken became restive. My going to India was the final blow. When I arrived in Kohat an apologetic letter explained that he could not tolerate Schroders Bank a minute longer while his younger brother was halfway to China. He was embarking on our journey alone. "I'll meet you in Samarkand," he wrote. More letters came, full of bizarre detail. He had walked through France, been befriended by a near criminal brothel keeper in Marseilles, and departed on the deck of a leaky tramp steamer to Athens. He was on the island of Mykonos, brushing up his modern Greek and making love to the maidens of Hellas, while I was suffering rejection in the Shalimar Gardens and picking my way painfully over the dangerous nastiness of the Kolohoi glacier.

For eighty rupees Billy and I bought an old American car, a Buick, with a soft top in terrible condition and other unpleasant features. It was hell to start and only expired some time after being switched off. It also had wheel wobble at speeds over thirty miles an hour. One Saturday in August we set out early for Peshawar and the Khyber Pass, a mini adventure which appealed to us both. For me it was a step towards Samarkand and the Silk Road, but Billy had serious worries about our vehicle.

"I don't believe this stupid car will climb the Kohat Pass," he grumbled. "Even if it does it'll blow up in the middle of the Peshawar Plain, and we'll have to return by camel."

The climb up the pass was, in fact, our most formidable obstacle. We laboured up the long inclines as the road traversed the hillside, getting steeper and more snakelike towards the summit. The radiator boiled just before we reached the top, and we parked by the roadside as the water cooled down, getting a fine view of the little town of Kohat and the cantonment, looking like an oasis in a brown desert. Cruising down on the other side, the wheel wobble began. Billy was driving and I could see him struggling for control as we veered towards a precipice.

"I was watching the speedometer," I said, as soon as we'd stopped. "At thirty miles an hour it was running fine. The thumping started when you reached forty on that long stretch." We drove on, agreeing to keep the speed below forty at all times, and we had no further trouble as we rattled and banged our way across the plain. Progress was slow anyway, because the road was crowded with mile-long camel trains from the north, their beasts loaded with carpets, on their way into the heart of India. Men, women and children walked in the dusty track beside the road, the men with patriarchal beards, the women proudly unveiled and handsome in their multi-coloured skirts, and the children usefully employed in guiding the camels. Such caravans must have been taking this route for a thousand years, perhaps much longer than a thousand years. In the bazaar at Peshawar I bought a camel rug from Bukhara which I still own. Unlike the old Buick, it was made to last several centuries and the colours have become more jewel-like with constant wear.

We then drove to Landi Kotal, the border post with Afghanistan. The Khyber Pass, which has seen the invading armies of Alexander the Great and Babur, is approached by a narrow defile. The rock face on either side is covered with the insignia of British and Indian regiments which guarded and sometimes fought here. The dates went back a hundred years, but were freshly painted and well maintained. I believe these touching memorials can still be seen preserved in their original glory by the government of Pakistan.

I had just one piece of good luck. A time-expired Wapiti had to be delivered to RAF Drigh Road, a maintenance depot near Karachi, for break up. I was probably chosen for the flight because the senior pilots thought it was a bore. The track followed the path of the Indus River to the sea, with one stop at Khanpur, a standard emergency landing ground on the edge of the Great Indian Desert. It was a flight of over six hundred miles, eight hours of precious flight time at an average ground speed of less than eighty miles an hour.

I had seen the Indus carving deep channels through the red rock at Attock and Kushalgarh, but here it spread out over the plain in numberless streams as far as the eye could see. Khanpur was a small town of the same neutral shade as the surrounding desert. The landing ground was the standard postage stamp square of, sunbaked mud—400 by 400 yards—with a white circle in the middle. To guard against flooding, an ominous ditch surrounded it, making me unusually aware that the Wapiti had no brakes. New experiences, like first love, make indelible impressions on the mind, and I will not forget landing at this lonely place in conditions of no wind, nervously getting my tail down close to the boundary and narrowly avoiding a ground loop short of the ditch. There was no motor transport to meet me. A single mud hut stood fifty yards from the field and two Indians with mud-coloured clothes brought tins of petrol in a bullock cart. I unscrewed the fuel tank for them and they poured in turn.

I ate the officers' mess sandwiches and watched the slow, careful movements of the Indians. Afterwards they spoke to me, but I didn't know enough Urdu to fully understand. One of the men had been given a camera by a visiting "RAF sahib." He showed it to me. I think he wanted film for it and imagined that sahibs who would give away such valuable objects would carry film on them at all times. I took off and circled the little town. The desert stretched on one side, the Indus plain on the other. I felt like a pioneer aviator, a lonely bird-man over immemorial India, the hot wind blowing in my face in the open cockpit. The journey was over before I could realize, grasp it. Eight hours of contemplation wasn't enough. All too soon the coast glimmered in the distance, and I saw the vast bulk of the airship hangar, built for the British dirigible R101, just south of the city.

I flew over Karachi before landing, a rose-red city in the evening sun. Streets of Victorian office buildings, motor traffic in the broad tree-lined avenues, tongas drawn by skinny horses, an Imperial Airways flying boat on the water, incongruously frail beside the tramp steamers and tankers in the harbour.

7

WAPITIS TO THE DEFENCE OF MADRAS
23rd August 1939 to 6th September 1939

Flight Lieutenant F.R.C. 'Chick' Fowle was our new flight commander—a blond heroic type with piercing blue eyes and a lick of golden hair. His tight-lipped style was a parody of military correctness and I took an immediate dislike to him. He reacted instinctively by giving me the job of officer in charge of pay, the most boring of squadron tasks and the most remote from flying. I despised the rituals of accounting and resented being reduced to a bank teller, a role I have been in panicky retreat from all my life. I had to type financial statements and Corporal Huntley, a young pay clerk who was soon to be flying bombers over Germany, was amused at my inefficiency.

> The typing of Mr Morley-Mower (he wrote)
> Could not be slower.
> I am unable to say
> How he became officer in charge of pay.

The section was run by a rubicund balding sergeant who I thought of as being completely honest. One day he urged me to count the cash before dispensing it to the airmen.

"Have you checked it yourself, sergeant?" I asked

"Oh, yes sir, I've checked it."

"Well, that's good enough for me."

"I think you should check it for yourself," he said, and added gravely, "You have to sign for it."

He couldn't persuade me to do so, and when all the airmen had been paid I was fifty rupees short. There was nothing I could say to the sergeant. He had covered himself completely, but he might just as well have picked my pocket. I knew I had to report the loss at once and I walked from the pay office to the station headquarters, fabricating excuses.

I never understood why Slim Olney became station adjutant. He had been a pilot in 60 Squadron (which I saw as halfway to heaven) and was now a full-time administrator, sitting behind a desk all day. Promotion may have depended on getting administrative experience, an idea that went out of the window as soon as the war started. He was a tall, fat man who had an air of world-weary efficiency. He was not sympathetic when I told him about the fifty rupees. He had a Charles Laughton accent to go with his Charles Laughton figure, and he reminded me of a dissolute Roman emperor in an old movie, consigning Christians to the Colosseum.

"My dear Em Em," he said, "you'll never learn. Rules are there because they make sense. Of course a pay officer has to count the cash! His signature is the final word. You'll just have to give me a cheque for fifty rupees to make it good. You probably don't have much money. I could leave it till the end of the month.."

"No, I've got the money."

"It'll teach you a lesson."

It was better than being torn to pieces by lions in an amphitheatre, but fifty rupees was a lot of cash in those days.

Billy Bowden was detached to Ambala to learn to fly the Bristol Blenheim, which was due to replace the Wapiti in light bomber squadrons. While he was away I languished on the ground at Kohat, having to beg for every flight. A technician in 'C' Flight drew a cartoon of me, a ball of frustration several feet above the ground, screaming, "I wanna fly! I wanna fly!" Chick Fowle was irritated at my constant requests and our relationship went from bad to worse.

above: Wapitis being refuelled at landing ground.
below: The author's Wapiti in flight. The pannier for bedrolls
and spare parts can be seen under the lower starboard wing.

Meanwhile the war grew closer. Chick paced up and down the tarmac in front of 'C' Flight hangar, barking orders like a ham actor. Vickers Valentias from 31 Squadron at Ambala began to come in to Kohat crammed with spares. The Valentia pilots loved their jobs, flying their cigar-shaped ugly biplanes all over the world—back and forth to the Middle East, dropping down to Habbaniya, Cairo, Beirut, Cyprus, always called up for any emergency in India, getting more air time than anyone else. I envied them their energy and professionalism, and wondered at their drinking habits—always at the bar at closing time and off at dawn the next day on another long adventure. Ken Mackie became a lifelong friend. He was a heavy drinker in those days, but his love of flying was his enduring intoxication and he never gave it up. When he got too old for the airlines he crop dusted in North Africa and New Zealand. Jimmy Chappell let me act as second pilot on a trip to Ambala on 26th August, and I enjoyed managing the clumsy craft, so heavy that its inertia caught me out at first. He let me try a landing and I found myself heaving at the stick like a navvy. As we climbed down from the high cockpit late that afternoon, war fever had reached a crisis.

Chick Fowle had just called a meeting of all personnel in the hangar. "'C' Flight," he announced in ringing tones, "has been deployed to Madras in southern India. The government wants a show of force. As soon as war breaks out Madras may be under attack from the east." I nearly burst out laughing. What could six old Wapitis with a top speed of eighty-five miles an hour do to defend the city of Madras?

"We will be flying over populated areas," he went on, "to give confidence to the citizens. All aircraft must be ready to take off by seven o'clock tomorrow morning."

Everyone worked till midnight. Panniers were fitted under the wings and stuffed with bedrolls and tool kits, lashed securely with rope and open to the weather. When we finally did take off at nine o'clock the air was already stifflingly hot and our aircraft were so heavily loaded that they used up the whole airfield to get their wheels off the ground, staggering into the air like overfed vultures. It took us some time to clear the little ring of hills, and then the Indus Plain stretched before us. Our track lay southeast, skirting the desert region, heading for the fertile Punjab, the granary of India. Chick wisely made little effort to gain height. We flew in loose formation at a thousand feet and an airspeed of 75 mph.

Amritsar, the city of the Sikhs, could be seen from far off, its domes and temples glittering in the sun. As we approached Chick waggled his wings, a sign to close the formation, (we had no other communication beyond the visual). Fighting the controls in the bumpy noon air I saw the Golden Temple with its fort-like outer walls and the blue waters of the holy pool. Some of the worshippers waved at us in support, or perhaps in anger at the profanation, for we descended to 500 feet and I could see the shadows of our planes racing over the houses.

We landed at Ambala just after one o'clock. The flight had taken four and a quarter hours. I worked out the ground speed as 87 mph, with a following wind! There was a line up of Bristol Blenheims beside the tower. It was the first time I had seen bombers of the current era, with their streamlined shapes and 'greenhouse' cockpits. Billy Bowden was there to meet us at the refuelling station.

"How do you like 'em?" I asked.

"Great!" he replied. "It's a different world. Retractable undercart. Variable pitch props. Lots of power. Double the speed of the old Wapiti." I didn't envy him. Whenever I thought of a Blenheim I had the gloomy image of flying that greenhouse over a defended enemy city with the murderous flak coming up at me in waves, and dropping bombs that would kill the innocent and me too.

The next leg of our journey was due south, and it turned out to be a guided tour of Mogul India at the speed of a modern

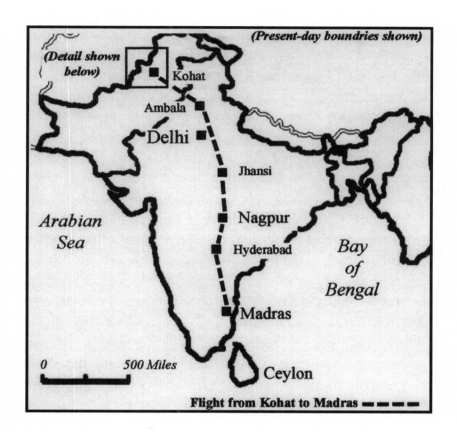

Route followed from Kohat to Madras.
Courtesy: Terrence Haney

helicopter. We passed over the Kutb Minar, an elaborately decorated tower dating from the 13th century which commemorated
the Moslem conquest. At Delhi we closed formation for a trium-
phal fly past of the Old Fort, with its massive red sandstone battlements. Following the line of the River Jumna, the Taj Mahal came
into view, and Chick dived us down to 500 feet again to salute it.
My gunner, Coggins, took a picture with my box Brownie camera. It shows in the foreground a piece of Wapiti wing and beyond
it the marble mausoleum, looking more like a palace with its rectangular pools and formal gardens. A little further on we saw the
most spectacular sight of all. On a steep cliff overlooking the plain
was the stronghold of Gwalior, which historically guarded routes
to the south. The Maharajah's eight palaces and artificial lakes
are contained within the walls of the fortress. The buildings, piled
up in ramshackle fashion like small cities, were reflected in the
waters, giving an impression of civilization and peace.

It was almost dark when we appeared over the small civil
airfield of Jhansi in Central India. The city, whose street lights
could be seen flickering below us, stood in the shadow of a hill
crowned by a 17th century castle. A line of oil lamp flares had
been laid out to indicate direction of landing and a lone green
Verey light rose, spluttered and fell. Fowle put his right hand on
the top of his helmeted head to order us into "line astern" formation. As the most junior pilot I landed last, surprised at the feel of
damp rich turf under my wheels after months of touching down
on dried mud.

An Indian cavalry regiment was stationed nearby and their
duty officer a pleasant fellow with a large moustache and a British
accent, welcomed us. Chick insisted on the aircraft being refuelled before we left the airfield, and by the time we had been trans-
ported five miles to his tradition-haunted mess, the communal
meal was long over. We ate in the empty dining room at a long
table that was over a hundred years old, its surface shining with
unnumbered polishings. Mess servants wearing elaborately folded

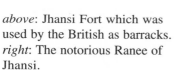

above: Jhansi Fort which was used by the British as barracks.
right: The notorious Ranee of Jhansi.
below: Coggin's photograph of the Taj Mahal with the Jumna River in the background.

turbans and immaculate uniforms moved silently and efficiently to anticipate our smallest needs. The mess silver was something to wonder at. The centrepiece was of a horseman with sabre drawn galloping into the mouth of an enemy cannon. Oil paintings of past colonels, framed accounts of acts of courage, heads of tigers and the horns of lesser beasts adorned the walls. It was in some respects a junk shop, for many of the objects were of value only to the regiment. I was taken on a tour of this military museum after dinner. The RAF certainly had nothing like it. Our traditions dated, by comparison, from the day before yesterday and our messes were often characterless and bare. Our units were always on the move, leaving few imprints on the buildings they once occupied. No flying station that I knew had an officers mess that remotely resembled this one.

We couldn't continue our flight the next day because the monsoon rains had temporarily flooded the landing grounds at Kamptee and Secunderabad. I spent the day looking around the old fort which commanded the countryside. In 1857 the Indian soldiers employed by the East India Company mutinied because of an unfounded rumour that the British cartridges they used were smeared with the fat of cows and pigs—the cow being sacred to the Hindu, and the pig being abominated by the Muslim. Taking advantage of the chaos, the Ranee of Jhansi, a woman of the fiercest character, carried out atrocities on the British community and held out in her fort against the troops which came to avenge them. The fortress was taken on the hottest day of the year and it is said that the soldiers discarded their red coats and fought half naked. The Ranee escaped disguised as a sepoy, but was killed by a British lancer ten miles from the fort.

> Diary entry: 28th August 1939
> Great view from the battlements over a flooded countryside. Inside the fort a nice Indian gentleman took me through the Hindu temple. It was dedicated to the elephant god Ganesa. Very strange and curiously dignified. I expected to laugh, but was impressed by the

atmosphere of simple piety. The statue of the god, with its elephant head and the body of a man was decorated with flowers. Rice and fruit was laid at its feet. I found myself thinking, "I like Hindus."

The Northwest Frontier had been overwhelmingly Muslim and this was my first opportunity to see a Hindu place of worship. And it was my first clear realization that there were two kinds of Indians and that perhaps Muslims worried me more. My brother officers favoured Muslims over Hindus. They thought of the Muslims as warriors and the Hindus as hucksters and money-lenders, in spite of the gallant record of the Punjabi, Sikh and Maratha regiments which fought on our side in the Great War. E.M. Forster is typically British in putting a noble Muslim at the centre of his *Passage to India*, and in making inordinate fun of the Hindu gentleman, Doctor Godbole, whose muddled religious thoughts are satirized. But I found something sympathetic about the temple at Jhansi, and it has stayed with me as a decisive impression.

The next day, the 29th of August, we rose before dawn to take the best advantage of a break in the weather. The plan was to make a dash for Madras in three hops of three and a half hours each, landing at the civil airports of Kamptee and Secunderabad for re-fuelling. It was a good idea, because monsoon rains annually produce floods unheard of in Europe. If we delayed, grass airfields might be unusable for weeks to come, trapping us in central India. In the half light of dawn the scene was already one of flooded fields and swollen rivers, whole areas of farmland being completely under water. The clouds were mercifully just above 1000 feet and the visibility was good at first, giving extraordinary views of drowned villages and their swarming, brightly clad inhabitants.

After an hour's flying the rain began and the cloud base lowered. Chick Fowle overshot Kamptee, misreading his map over an altered countryside, but he eventually led us over the airfield which was scarcely recognizable as a landing area. It seemed more like a rectangular swamp with the concrete circle looking like a lifeboat in the middle of it. He landed first and fired a green Verey to order us to follow him in. His Wapiti had come to a rapid stop after touching down, which I judged to be excellent flying technique, but we all had 'carrier landing' arrivals, our main wheels sending up sheets of water and our heavy metal tailskids biting into the waterlogged turf.

There was no possibility of continuing in such conditions, and we were stuck at Kamptee for the next two days. No accomodation had been reserved and we spent one night lying on damp bed rolls in the tiny airport hangar. On August 31st there was a clearance and we took off before midday for Secunderabad, a city nestled against its twin city of Hyderabad, then ruled as an independent state by the Nizam of Hyderabad. He was said to be the richest man in the world and had recently donated a destroyer to the Royal Navy. After re-fueling we flew in tight formation over the palace of this potentate, a castellated citadel with thirteen gates. I had an image in my mind of His Highness, looking up from his silken couch to see the armed might of the Royal Air Force as it reached a speed of ninety miles an hour in a slight dive!

As we passed down the Velikonda Range the cloud lifted and we circled Madras in late afternoon sunshine. After securing the aircraft we bundled into taxis and headed for the city centre where accomodations had been reserved, mostly in small hotels. Chick and Bum Thomas being senior, were housed at the military club. I was allotted a room at the top of an office building. It was nicely furnished and had an outlook on the busy street below, but I had no contact with the other pilots and we were not meeting as a group until the next day. So that night I wandered out alone into my first Indian city, and I was unprepared for the experience.

There is a concentration of horror at the heart of Western cities; drug addicts, street walkers, bag ladies and people who sleep above metal grids in winter, keeping warm in the smelly air exhausted from office buildings. In India the sights are far worse.

above: The Tiger Moth I flew at Madras.
below: The author in front of his Blenheim at Ambala, October 1939.

The first beggar I saw was young, perhaps sixteen, his twisted limbs decked out in rags, shuffling along the pavement like a crab, holding his bowl up to the sky and crying for alms. An old man covered with sores who seemed to have lost his mind was chanting in a hoarse voice, looking upward with blind eyes. There were women, too, with gaunt black faces, sometimes holding skeletal children in their arms. And this desperate unhappiness was not in a backstreet but among the hotels and offices of the city centre. I took refuge in the Killarney Hotel—an incongruous note I have not invented—a grey Victorian edifice with a lounge filled with British people in evening dress. An orchestra was playing a selection from Noel Coward's "Cavalcade," and clean and powdered ladies were showing bare backs as they danced with their partners on the raised platform of the dance floor. The hotel was air conditioned, something unknown on the Northwest Frontier, and unknown to me at the time. The shock of cold air was unexpected and unnerving.

I ordered a Pimm's No. 1 cocktail and then another, feeling as alien to this comfortable hell as I did to the less comfortable hell outside the hotel's swing doors. A war was about to begin without me. Ken and Peter would join up and I would be dressing for dinner and flying antique aircraft in perfect safety thousands of miles from the fighting. Even that issue paled in the light of the human suffering on the street. The more I drank the more tragic life seemed. As I rose to go I knew that I was drunk. When the hot air hit me I lost my legs and was rescued by a taxi driver who took me by the arm and led me through the waiting beggars to his cab.

He was an Anglo-Indian gentleman with a very black skin whose name was Yardley. He proudly pointed out the inscription on his cab, 'Yardley's Taxi Service.' He identified himself as a loyal supporter of the Old Country in its time of peril. I admitted drunkenly that I was one of the band of heroes who had arrived that day to defend his native city.

"Sir," he said, "we Britons will give a good account of ourselves." He looked at first glance entirely Indian, but there was an English coarseness about his short nose, and his grandfather's pale eyes stared incongruously out of his dark face. Some Victorian redcoat, living with a native woman where his regiment was stationed, had fathered a line of Yardleys who were still loyal to the crown with their diminishing supply of white blood. There must have been some item in the local newspaper about our "reinforcement" of the city, for he seemed to know more about the reason for our presence than I did. He chatted non-stop in a singsong voice, deliberating wisely on Hitler's threat to the civilized world.

"We cannot tolerate," he said pontifically, "a German hogmanay in Europe." He meant hegemony, but it was a good try. Drunk as a Scotsman and sad as an Assyrian, I laughed weakly at this slip of the tongue. It was the only bright spot in the evening.

On 2nd September 1939, we did a demonstration flight over the city and Chick assembled the pilots and crews to explain the significance of this event which, according to him, was to leave the vivid air signed with our honour. There was strong wind from the north and scattered clouds were moving fast at 2000 feet. We formed up over the airfield to the south of the town and followed Mount Road towards the business district, over Island Ground, the Gymkhana Club and Fort St George, a stubby monument that was the first British trading post of the East India Company in the 17th century. Dead into wind, we moved a little faster than the traffic on the road beneath us. However, we turned around on the northern outskirts and roared over the Killarney Hotel at 120 miles an hour on the way back. I was confident that Mr Yardley was watching us with pride and satisfaction.

The newspapers that day had banner headlines, "Hitler Invades Poland," and a declaration of war by Mr. Chamberlain was expected. I retired to my lonely room that evening and mulled over the weirdness and the moral discomfort of being in Madras, of all places, when the world was going up in flames on my own doorstep. What a fantasy to be fighting the Germans once again! When I was fourteen, Ken and I had spent two weeks in Bavaria. We had marched from the railway station at Munich southwards to Berchtesgaden stopping every night at a village where often there was no inn; or if there was it was too expensive for us. We were doing the whole holiday on twenty pounds sterling, including the Dover-Calais ferry and the train fare to Munich. Part of our enjoyment was managing our slender resources. We knocked at the humbler doors and asked, *"Haben Sie Zimmer fuer eine Mark Zvanzig, bitte?"* We never failed to get good lodgings. The Germans seemed a sunny, clean and healthy people and they welcomed English boys with enthusiasm. In the Jugendherberge at Berchtesgaden, where good plain accomodation was available for one Mark a night, we were feted by a dormitory of youngsters our own age, dressed like boy scouts, swastika armbands on their sleeves and daggers in their stockings. They were all going to see the Fuehrer at his mountain eyrie, and they urged us to go with them. "The Fuehrer would be especially pleased to see English boys," they said. I would have liked to go but Ken wanted to climb the Zugspitze. Anyway we thought of Hitler as a Charlie Chaplin figure, gesticulating with that absurd salute, so we climbed the Zugspitze instead. How could I be fighting these amiable people who held us in such esteem? I had read Remarque's *All Quiet on the Western Fron*t and I knew Germans hated war as much as we did.

On 3rd September war was declared with Germany. It made a thudding noise in my brain but I shook it off to spend the evening watching an Indian film. The central character was an Anglicized Hindu gentleman with a large moustache who wore Western clothing and ordered servants around in a parody of the British official. He falls in love with a beautiful maiden who converts him to the struggle for Indian nationhood. At the conclusion he is clean shaven, dressed in white Ghandi homespun, and leading a procession of wildly enthusiastic villagers to overthrow British rule.

On 4th September I flew my first offensive sortie of the war. Chick, without a smile, sent me on a "shipping reconnaissance" down the coast to the French colonial city of Pondicherry, which looked smaller than I'd imagined from its dramatic appearance in English history. In 1746, its governor, Joseph Dupleix, marched north to capture Madras for the French crown. However, a year later the treaty of Aix-la-Chapelle gave it back to Great Britain in exchange for Nova Scotia. I enjoyed the flight, admired this outpost of imperial France, but saw no shipping.

There was a flying club on the Madras airfield, and the flying instructor, a meek balding gentleman of middle age, bore the name of Tyndale-Biscoe, a family famous for Anglican bishops and imperial administrators. I wondered why he was there, so far from home, employed in such a humble profession. He didn't have the air of a drunk or a remittance man. Had he been with the Royal Flying Corps in the early days of aviation? Was he romantically clinging to the enthusiasms of his youth? Did he have some private vice that could be safely practiced in South India? I asked him if I could fly the club Tiger Moth and he checked me out with one landing. I flew for an hour, sightseeing and performing aerobatics over the ocean. It was absurd to pay good money to fly, when I was in an operational flying squadron, and getting airborne every day. It was partly loneliness and partly frustration. I justified it in my own mind by saying that I had added a new type to my log book, though a Tiger Moth was not worth acquiring. I wanted to ask Mr Tyndale-Biscoe why he was in Madras and what his history was, but something about his patrician reserve, or perhaps his august name, prevented me.

Fowle briefed me for another patrol on 6th September, this time up the coast to Pulicat, a small port 100 miles north of Madras. He put on his standard dramatic performance.

"Look out for and describe any significant shipping," he said fiercely. "Keep your eyes open for enemy aircraft and, of course, for subs." By this time rage was my predominant emotion. The absurd assignment I could have swallowed, but the last reel Gary

Cooper pose was too much. He was speaking as if the Germans were seriously planning to invade India via the Madras beaches and would soon be goose-stepping past the Killarney. I blew away my frustration by scorching up the shoreline at low level. It was a gorgeous day, the sea and sky being an almost identical shade of blue. The narrow strip of white sand was for many miles totally deserted and the jungle rose behind it like a green wall. Parrots climbed in green confusion as I rushed by. An occasional fishing village with its cluster of boats made me curious enough to circle and observe. The settlements looked fragile and temporary, the houses half hidden by the palm jungle. Blackskinned figures rushed down to the beach, waving hands in the air, mouths open in wonder at having their solitude disturbed by my old-fashioned flying contraption. I did not bother about ships or submarines. This was pure flying, pure liberty.

Pulicat was nothing much. A larger clearing in the trees and a small harbour. I remember thinking, "I wouldn't swop this for a flying boat," but I was lying to myself. I'd have loved settling down on the water near Pulicat, dropping anchor and watching the fleet of light craft paddling out to welcome me. Some dreams die hard.

When I landed back, Bum Thomas was on the tarmac waving a piece of paper above his head and grinning like a monkey.

"Good news for you," he shouted. "A signal's just come in from Air Headquarters. You're off to Ambala for Blenheim training. You're to leave on the night train."

"Whoopee!"

I wasn't as pleased as I sounded. I believed the rumour—which turned out to be true—that 27 Squadron was being re-equipped for the defence of Singapore. That was not my preferred direction. I thought of Singapore as one of the safest places on the planet, surrounded by water and under the protection of the Royal Navy. I was convinced the war would end quickly in the West, that my brothers would distinguish themselves in battle, and that I, the professional airman, would miss the thing entirely.

8

BACK TO THE TOCHI RIVER
6th September 1939 to 25th December 1939

The Indian railway system is one of the wonders of the orient. Some bewhiskered Victorian genius had opted for a wider gauge than the British one and the compartments were more roomy. My kit, which included a gramaphone and a case of records, fitted easily under the two bench seats, wide as single beds and just as comfortable. Air conditioning was unheard of outside the large metropolitan hotels, but ice was available in huge slabs which the railway servants placed in metal containers on the floor. Electric ceiling fans were then directed downwards, bouncing cool air off the ice and distributing it throughout the compartment. There were no dining cars but something far better was arranged. Officials passed through the carriages asking passengers when they wished to eat and what they required. A message would then be telegraphed up the line. When the train drew in to the designated station, a uniformed servant would be waiting with a trolley filled with covered dishes. He would enter the compartment and set out the plates, cutlery and napkins, remaining in attendance while the meal was eaten. After clearing up he alighted with his paraphernalia at the next stop and waited for a down train to return him to his point of origin. I thought it was a lordly procedure, and the food was always excellent. The ice container in my compartment leaked, and when I arrived at Ambala water covered the floor. I thought nothing of it, but when I looked at my gramaphone records they were warped and ruined. I had a collection of Benny Goodman, The Hot Club of France, Louis Armstrong, Chopin piano pieces and late Beethoven string quartets. Never replaced.

Ambala was something of an anti-climax. Billy had already returned to Kohat so there was no one to exchange ideas with. I flew a total of five hours and ten minutes on Blenheims, instructed by Squadron Leader McKechnie, no longer the CO of 27 Squadron. He had been a flying instructor in his younger days and was now thoroughly enjoying himself at his old job. Wing Commander Dick Ubee,[1] a much respected ex-test pilot, was the station commander and he co-opted me to play squash with him every evening. He was a very cunning player and I was of the wild and sweaty school. We had some wonderful games, which left me exhausted and he victorious.

The Bristol Blenheim was an advanced modern light bomber and very different from the underpowered boxkites I had been flying, but it didn't attract me in the least. Wapitis and Hawker Hart variants had an aura of romance about them. The very sight of them, propped up expectantly on their fixed undercarriages, told of the pioneer days of aviation. The Blenheim seemed characterless. Aerobatics and even violent maneuvers were forbidden, so the course consisted of circuits and bumps and flying around with one engine shut down. After a week spent hanging around the locker room reading *Pilots Notes*, or carrying out simulated instrument flying on the Link Trainer, I returned to Kohat by train.

---

[1] Dick Ubee had a distinguished career and was one of the most universally popular of all the RAF officers in my time. He was the first commandant of the RAF Flying College, Manby, where, in spite of having lost one eye in a flying accident, he routinely thrashed me on the squash court after work. He retired in 1958 as an air vice marshal.

The station was in confusion, units and people on the move and rumours abounding. Many of the senior pilots had departed to England. 60 Squadron was packing up, scheduled for re-equipment at Ambala and by rumour headed east. Billy had been transferred and was going with them. Just before Christmas 28 Squadron began to move in, taking the hangar space, the technical sections, the barracks and the officers quarters being vacated by 60 Squadron. It was an army co-operation unit flying Hawker Audaxes and had previously been located at Fort Sandeman to the southwest of the province. To this squadron I was transferred, thus altering the whole course of my life.

This was the period of the 'phoney war.' Britain had sent an expeditionary force to France, but it did not have a single armoured division. Much to everyone's surprise there was no fighting on the Western Front. Winston Churchill called the silence of the guns "a sinister trance." Poland had been rapidly crushed and partitioned between Russia and Germany. Stalin, having signed a non-aggression pact with Hitler, was quietly absorbing the Baltic states and engulfing the Finns. It was the lull before the storm, but most people thought the war would fizzle and become a stalemate.

"It's going to be a flop," Billy said to me, as we watched the 60 Squadron motor transport, crammed with tool boxes and disgruntled airmen, disappear in clouds of dust through the tree-lined avenues of the cantonment. "Only the squadrons in England will see some action. The boys with white gloves, you know. We're too far away. It'll all be over by the summer. We're going to miss the whole damned show."

"Hitler may be biding his time," I offered.

Billy laughed bitterly. "If he really intended to attack France, he'd have done it by now. Believe me, you're going to spend the war dropping twenty-pounders on empty hillsides in Waziristan, while I'm sitting in the Singapore Yacht Club drinking gin slings and waiting for something to happen. It's just our luck."

At this point Billy Bowden disappears from my narrative. I was at Miramshah for months on end, and when I returned to Kohat he was in Malaya. 27 Squadron flew into Sungei Patani in Northern Malaya on 17th February 1940. Chick Fowle took command of the unit less than a year later. On 8th December 1942, the squadron was effectively wiped out on the ground and in the air by the Japanese Air Force. Remembering Bum Thomas' kindness and his warm personality I hate to think that he might have perished in a Japanese prisoner of war camp, along with John Manton, Logger Powley, Chokra Crystal and others. Not to mention my air gunner, Coggins, who took the snapshot of the Taj Mahal. Chick Fowle must have survived the experience, because it is recorded that he was promoted to wing commander and awarded a Distinguished Flying Cross, perhaps in another operational theatre.

Billy Bowden was another matter. I worried continuously about his fate and tried to discover what had happened to him, without success. By an extraordinary chance I met him in 1946. We passed one another in a corridor of the Air Ministry, Adastral House, London. I recognized him at once and stopped him. He looked thinner, but had the same mischievous embarrassed smile.

"How'd you get out of Singapore?" I asked, assuming that he had somehow avoided that horror. "I worried about you being a prisoner."

"It's a long story," Billy said. "Too long to be told now."

"Where are you off to? Can't we have lunch?"

"I'm sailing for Canada tomorrow. And I'm rushing for an interview. I'll write you." We exchanged addresses and parted.

An amazingly detailed account of the chaos surrounding the fall of Singapore was published in 1992. 1 looked in the index for names and found Billy Bowden right off. He had apparently transferred to No. 60 Squadron and had been shot down in a Blenheim while attacking enemy shipping off Singapore.

F/L W.E. Bowden's L4913 was hit, the Canadian
pilot attempting to ditch the stricken aircraft, which
broke up on impact; Bowden emerged as the only survivor, supporting himself on the aircraft's tailwheel until
picked up by a Japanese destroyer after 24 hours in
the sea, thereby gaining the dubious distinction of
being the first Allied airman to be taken prisoner by
the Japanese.[2]

So Billy had spent four years in a Japanese prisoner of war
camp! And survived! What stories of humiliation, torture and dep-
rivation could he have told? Did he slave, half naked and starving
on the Railway of Death? Or was he carried back to Tokyo as a
trophy? Was he tied to a wooden bench on his back and flogged
on his chest and stomach with a heavy stick, like the Scot, Eric
Lomax?[3] Was he caged like a beast, living in his own excrement
for weeks on end? Did he end up in Changi gaol, sixty pounds
underweight and covered with sores, lucky to be alive when VJ
Day arrived? I thought I would never know, for Billy did not write
to me and I lost touch with him forever. However, in 1998 I heard
from Lester Davies[4] that he had met Billy in 1945 and heard part
of his story. Apparently he was well treated by the Japanese sail-
ors who had picked him out of the sea; but after he was handed
over to the Japanese army he was subjected to torture so severe
and prolonged that he was often close to death. My imaginations
had not been far off the mark.

When told I was no longer a member of 27 Squadron but
now belonged to an alien unit, I was upset. I had no objection to
flying Audaxes, but it had been the custom of 27 Squadron to

---

[2] Christopher Shore and Brian Cull, with Yasuho Izawa, *Bloody Shambles*.
Grub Street, London, 1992, Vol. I, pp 88-89.
[3] Eric Lomax, *The Railway Man*. W.W. Norton & Co., New York, 1995,
pp. 143-4.
[4] Lester Davies was involved with the ground war in Malaysia and wrote
about his adventures in, *The Sun Set in the East*.

look down on army co-operation pilots. They were below the salt, compromised by their subordination to the army. At flying school we had been lectured on the importance of an independent air arm, as theorized by Lord Trenchard, the 'Father of the Royal Air Force' and its first Commander-in-Chief. Throughout most of World War I it had been called the Royal Flying Corps, but Trenchard, by his strong personality and conviction, had persuaded the politicians to separate it from the army. It was a stroke of genius. Trenchard believed that the bomber would be the decisive weapon in future wars and its campaign must not be tied to the battlefield. If the Germans had adopted the same scheme they might have won the war swiftly in 1939. As it was, they developed battlefield aircraft like the Stuka, to terrorize undefended cities and support ground troops. Afterwards they built a huge fighter force and were like a boxer, nimble on his feet for defense, but unable to strike a knockout blow.

I soon found that the army co-op boys had developed their own feelings of superiority. Wilf Surplice, a tall balding Flight Lieutenant was the first to show me where I stood.

"You bomber boys don't know anything," he said. "We quite appreciate that. We have to take you as you are, but you'll have to learn fast."

He smiled when he said this. Surplice wasn't a bad chap, but lofty in more ways than one. And he was senior. He had more than a thousand hours in his log book. Having only a couple of hundred myself the thousand hour figure seemed dreamlike. I couldn't help envying him and looking up to him.

"Army co-op people not only do as much bombing as you bomber boys do, they have this relationship with the army. We patrol roads to keep them clear of road blocks, we cover picquets when a regiment withdraws. We keep accurate logs of our sorties on a knee pad. We keep touch with the people on the ground by picking up messages. All this is Greek to you, I'm afraid. In this squadron you're just a bog rat again."

above: Wing Commander Crowe, station commander at Kohat,
and his adjutant in front of a 28 Squadron Audax.
below: An Audax being 'bombed up.'

So it turned out. Looking at my log book, I see that I was signed out as a member of 27 Squadron on 16th December 1939. Two days later Wing Commander Crowe, the Kohat station commander, gave me a flight check on a 28 Squadron Audax. He let me do two landings, flight time twenty minutes, and then sent me solo. On the same day 28 Squadron flew in formation to Miramshah, and I with them in the back seat of 'Jacko' Jackson's aircraft. Jacko was the recently appointed squadron commander, a burly serious man who spoke a few words of welcome to me before take off.

"I'm sure you were looking forward to flying Blenheims, Morley," he said. "Fact is we need pilots. This emergency situation on the frontier. We'll be re-equipping with Lysanders soon. Specially designed for this type of work. You'll enjoy them when they arrive."

It was a partial apology for yanking me out of 27 Squadron and I appreciated it. I had seen photographs of Westland Lysanders. They were high wing monoplanes with heavy struts, sitting up on fixed undercarts. No, thank you! But Jacko was right about one thing. The frontier was in turmoil. The Wazirs had seen the opportunity of a lifetime to make trouble while the British were otherwise occupied. Road blocks and ambushes were everyday occurrences. The Bannu Brigade and the Tochi Scouts were finding it difficult to keep the roads open. The government had responded by selecting two areas for punitive proscription, the Karesta and Bhittani. They were both close to the Afghan border. When I arrived at Miramshah leaflets had already been dropped warning the tribesmen to remove their cattle and personal property.

From this time onward my log book becomes crowded. The restriction on the use of fuel which had made my life so miserable throughout 1939 was dropped, and everyone flew like mad. The next day, the 19th of December, Wilf Surplice took me as a passenger on a sortie over the Karesta, dropping two 112-pound bombs. This was exciting but nauseating, because dive bombing, so thrilling for the pilot, is stomach-wrenching for the man in the rear seat. After this we dropped mail to three of the Tochi forts, Ghariom, Bichi Kaskai and Datta Khel. My job was to throw out the weighted sacks while Surplice maneuvered his plane over the courtyard of the fort. It was crazy flying. The Tochi posts were castellated mud and brick strongholds, built to command a view of the countryside and the strategic roads. They were perched on minor eminences, sometimes overlooking river bridges or tucked into the sides of precipices. They preferred to have the mail tossed inside the walls, not wishing to face random fire from a sniper behind a rock on a nearby hill. This often meant dropping while the aircraft was in a turn, avoiding a rockface. The pilot had to fly slowly, not much above the stall, to give the mail dropper the best chance of making an accurate drop. I found myself standing up in the rear cockpit and hurling the packages into the slipstream, so that they could travel forward a little before descending. The lighter the package the better chance it had of slapping against the tailplane. It was the best fun I'd ever had as a passenger. The turbanned soldiers stood in little groups up against the walls, staring upwards and rushing for the bags as they neared the ground. I saw one man flattened by a heavy sack of mail; but he jumped up and ran off with it. I had been told the story of a 28 Squadron pilot who dropped a birthday cake in a tin for the fort commander, a present from his wife in Bannu. A soldier ran for it and took it square on the chin, like a knockout blow in the boxing ring. Luckily, after recovering consciousness he was found to be not seriously injured.

On our return to Miramshah, Surplice took advantage of a bright, windless day to pull off a neat tail-up landing, filling me with professional envy. I had been on starvation rations for a year and I had not dared to try any fancy flying since the accident at Kohat. Sitting behind him, feeling the masterful way he sashayed down the fort wall, his port wing flirting with the solitary tree outside the main gate, I swore that I would one day reach his level of expertise. I had already forgotten the faraway war, and was back to my dream of flying as pure art.

News of the phoney war did reach me, however. Ken wrote of his adventures getting back to Britain from Mykonos. He'd taken a tramp steamer to Taranto in southern Italy, but had no money left. So he began walking north, telling his story to all and sundry, begging food from the villages as he went. The Italians were wonderfully supportive, touched by his desire to return to the defence of his native land. Soon he was escorted to a railway station like a conquering hero, where officials were persuaded to wink at payment. Italy did not declare war on the Allies until June 1940, or he would certainly have been arrested and spent five years in a prisoner of war camp.

On 22nd December 1939, Shackels Majumdar flew in my back seat to give me a guided tour of the Tochi River forts, eight in all, map reading for me and telling stories about the seconded Indian Army officer who commanded each post, his age, rank, wife's name, sexual attractiveness and any scandal attached.

"You see Kar Kama." Shackels voice over the Gosport tubes.

"Yes." It was a neat little castle, three hundred yards from the white sand of a dried water course.

"There's no white cross," I shouted.

"Then fly as slowly as you can over the courtyard. I have a huge parcel here for Captain Jenkins. His wife Peggy lives in Bannu and worries herself sick about him. Beautiful girl. But she thinks he'll starve to death on Tochi food!"

Shackels was a small man. He had released his straps so that he could reach for the packages which crammed the rear cockpit. It required a mighty effort to throw the heavier ones out, and he looked as if he might throw himself out too. He was the perfect companion and I'd have hated to lose him. It would have been fun enough listening to him in an armchair at the club or in the officers mess. As it was, the conditions were idyllic, and I flew low and slow over the enchanting complexity of the river valley, laughing at Shackels' chatter as I circled the forts to drop their mail. If I could cite just one sortie to represent the glory of flight it would be this one, as I flew, conscious of the poetry of our antique open cockpit biplane, swooping and hovering like some clumsy buzzard over the wilderness of the Afghan border.

On the morning of 24th December, Wilf Surplice gathered his flight together in the sandbagged flight tent by the main gate of the fort. All the pilots were present, and the senior NCO's as well. It was standing room only in the confined and rather gloomy space; but Wilf was in a good mood as he sat on top of his desk, swinging his long legs.

"Jacko," he began, and then corrected himself, "Squadron Leader Jackson is going back to Kohat for a family Christmas, but he's given permission for a raid on Manzai. 5 Squadron has a detachment there commanded by our good friend Batts Barthold. We're going to surprise them early Christmas morning. Toilet rolls have been requisitioned and also bags of flour. To surprise them, we will take off at six oclock tomorrow, drop our real bombs on the Bhittani as per contract, and then proceed to drop our jokey bombs on Manzai."

A cheer went up. Nothing pleases childish minds like a Christmas hoax.[5] Surplice began to allot specific tasks but I was

---

[5] This sort of prank is part of service life and usually takes place when there is genuine friendship between the participants. While I was O.C. Flying at RAF Kinloss in Scotland in 1955, we were close enough to the Royal Naval Air Station at Lossiemouth to do a lot of partying together. I had a special friendship with Commander Robert McWhirter, the O.C. Flying there. One night he and his merry men broke into our officers mess and stole all our mess silver. Our reply was to invade Lossiemouth by night and to plant a fifty-foot fir tree at the intersection of their runways. I remember flying our station commander, Ronny Thomson, over to Lossiemouth at dawn to view the scene and to take incriminating photographs. We had painted the main runway with the inscription in giant letters, "CAPTAIN SPARE THAT TREE!"

above: This was RNAS Station Lossiemoth's first strike. The marauders painted their advertisment on the runway and then raided our officers' mess for the mess silver.   *below*: Our response was to plant a tree at the intersection of their main runways. The inscription says, "Captain Spare That Tree!"

excused because I was a stranger to the squadron. Also I had a sortie to fly that morning. The pilots of the five aircraft formation that carried out the Christmas raid were Wilf Surplice (leading), Bill Traill, a senior flight lieutenant with a large black moustache, Peter ap Ellis, whose father was a group captain in England, and a pig-faced officer named Stott, an unpleasant soldier-of-fortune type who had once served in the Palestine Police—and myself. Captain Frizelle, a fat clever Indian Army officer who shared liaison duties with Majumdar, flew with Surplice. Shackels flew with me.

Just after 6 am on Christmas Day Surplice led us in a formation take off. We were out of practice and there was much jostling for position and near collision. But we closed up for the long climb in steady air and soon made a respectable pattern against the dawn sky.

It took twenty minutes to reach the proscription area and I saw little of the countryside as I stared at Peter ap Ellis' tailplane, trying to keep my port wing tucked in close. Once over the Bhittani, Surplice gave the hand signal to break formation. He then turned to port in a wide circle, clearly searching for a target. We followed our leader, waiting for him to make the first dive. It was a desolate scene, without any mark of human habitation. Not a tower, not a castellated dwelling, not a stone wall circle for sheep. At this time of year it didn't look grazeable; just brown rock and dry gullies. Perhaps in the springtime some green shoots would appear. Suddenly Surplice climbed steeply and wheeled over in an Immelmann turn. We saw his plane heading vertically downwards.

What was he aiming at?

There was nothing, absolutely nothing to damage or destroy here; no human activity to harrass. Could there have been Wazirs hiding among the rocks? I doubted it. They were miles away in some more fruitful valley lower down on the range.

As soon as the 112-pounder raised its cloud of red dust on the ground, we could see that he had targeted the intersection of two dry water courses, the whiteish stones standing out against the prevailing ochre. It was an extremely useless exercise, but after all it was Christmas and we had something more amusing planned. When the last bomb was dropped, Surplice, tall in the cockpit, put his right hand above his helmeted head and waggled his wings slowly, the signal to close formation.

Forty minutes later we were approaching Manzai, a smaller version of Miramshah with a smaller landing ground. Unlike Miramshah it was not overloooked by a hill from which tribesmen could shoot at parked aircraft, so the 5 Squadron detachment's aircraft were sitting dispersed outside the fort walls. We had achieved total surprise. The fort gates were closed and there was no wisp of smoke to suggest human activity.

The first attack was made with the flour bombs. My aircraft was last in line and I watched while the others swept over the fort, the bombs making white streaks on the ground , on the fort walls and occasionally breaking in mid air to form a descending cloud.

"Bombs ready," Shackels shouted exitedly through the Gosport tubes.

"Let 'em go," I shouted back, gliding low over the fort. I could see the pilots running around in their pyjamas on the battlements and airmen pouring out of their tents below. The bombs had made an innocuous mess of their Christmas morning.

The second attack was with toilet rolls, inscribed with Christmas blessings, which uncurled in the bright air, spreading and twisting as they fell. When my turn came the fort was already draped with white, broken, fluttering strips of paper.

We circled awhile, savouring the scene of confusion, until Wilf Surplice called us in to tight formation for a final victorious f ly over.

My diary entry for 25th December 1940, concludes;

> Wildly amusing! Very very juvenile! I flew another
> bombing sortie over the Karesta in the afternoon. Too
> tired to enjoy the Christmas party in the mess.

9

THE KIDNAPPING
OF MAJOR DUGGAL
26th December 1939 to 25th January 1940

Two days after Christmas 1939, Major Duggal, a physician in the Indian Army Medical Corps was taken prisoner by a gang of tribesmen from the Shabi Khel. He had been driving across tribal territory with a red cross painted on his staff car. He was performing surgery and giving other medical services to the people. Passing from village to village and being often welcomed as a saviour, he may have felt himself immune to the historic dangers. The sick people he attended were grateful but others sought revenge. Two squadrons of aircraft were already punishing the people of Bhittani and Karesta for their roadblocking and ambushing of military convoys; and even though proscription was designed to kill no one, it must have been seen as an intolerable form of bullying. Major Duggal was not skinned alive like the unfortunate infantry officer but his captors demanded a large sum of money for his release. The Indian government refused to be blackmailed by criminals. RAF reinforcements were called up to punish the Shabi Khel Wazirs and force Duggall's captors to return him. Duggal's wife—who Shackels in his gossipy way reported as being very pretty—was outraged by the heartlessness of officialdom and, after raising money from her husband's brother officers, she set out on a tour of the cantonments at Peshawar, Kohat and Risalpur to raise more. Meanwhile Miramshah buzzed with military activity.

I took considerable interest in this emotional issue, believing the lovely Mrs Duggal was unlikely to see her husband again except as a violated corpse, and my diary of the period is more detailed than usual. Three Vickers Valentias from 11 Squadron flew into Miramshah on 1st January 1940. They were too large to pass the gates of the fort and had to be flown back to the safety of Kohat each night.

> Diary entry: 2 January 1940
> After my sortie over the Karesta this morning I flew over to the Shabi Khel to see what was going on. Three Valentias carrying eight 250 lb bombs apiece were flying to and fro like clockwork, knocking down what buildings remain in this high and remote area. The sight was amazing. The steep valley was filled with smoke and the big slow Valentias were crisscrossing on their individual approaches to the.targets, if you can call them targets. There really aren't any such. It's just a grazing area. Intelligence reports that the herdsmen moved out of the valley some days ago.

We were kept up to date on the situation every evening by Major Cobb and his staff. All the available officers traipsed through the fort to the P.A.'s quarters, and Frizelle and Shackels read the intelligence reports. They didn't amount to much. Rumours from the Khassadars, the tribal police force, that Duggal had been taken across the border into Afghanistan. That he was imprisoned in a cave high up on the Shabi Khel. That he had been tortured and his body disposed of. That the Faqir of Ipi had exerted his authority and the major was safe in his hands. They read a government memo expressing an implacable resolve not to accede to the demands of the kidnappers. Then Major Cobb would lecture us on the folly of British rule.

"The government doesn't know what it's doing," he would say, walking up and down, dropping his head and jerking it up again as he spoke. "They have no notion of the kind of people they are dealing with. I've had a decade of experience here and they won't even ask for my advice. The only way to get poor Duggal back is to bribe the maliks. They know where he's being kept and they know who's captured him. They'll hand over some of the money to the gang, and he'll be returned. As it is the army is on the move again, and this will play into the hands of extremists. There will be more road blocks, more army casualties, more reprisals. I've nothing against you air force chaps, but you'll do no good by bombing. It just hardens their hearts. If it goes on too long they may decide to take it out on Duggal. That's what I'm afraid of. I know these people."

I walked back one night through the dark corridors talking to Loppy Lerwill. In spite of his bearlike appearance he had a disconcerting lisp, pronouncing his r's in a liquid Germanic fashion, like a Ruritanian prince in a black-and-white movie. He was a good man, though. He could run all day over the toughest territory, and he prided himself on tiring out his best Tochis.

"What's going to happen, Loppy?" I asked.

"There's gossip among my people that a deal has already been struck for a lesser sum. I'd rather believe them than old Cobb. They have contacts in the villages, and the word is that the maliks have got together. What they call a *jirga*, a tribal meeting. That means only one thing. They're going to put pressure on the gang. Why would they meet if no government money had been offered?"

"Sounds good," I said.

"If you want to know what's going on around these parts, ask a Tochi!" We both laughed.

On 8th January I flew an early morning patrol ahead of the Bannu Brigade, which was clearing a road for the passage of a convoy. There was snow on the hills above Razmak and the usually harsh landscape looked almost pretty. The cold temperature made the air smooth and I flew low over the road as it snaked up passes, ran through gorges and followed river beds. Low flying was justified. The tribesmen would often choose a portion of the road where rocks overhung or where they could position themselves along a knife edge ridge. In this way they could attack without being observed, and having done their work they could disperse before being engaged.

On this day there were no ominous piles of rocks blocking traffic and when I landed back at Miramshah I reported the road clear. It was, however, under ambush. As the convoy approached a village called Latambar, a group of tribesmen opened fire on the last lorry, which contained Sikh troops. Of the twenty-six soldiers in the vehicle ten were killed outright and six were seriously injured. The gang, who had been concealed on both sides of the road, stole the rifles of the dead and wounded and made off up a steep hill to the north. Two of the ambushers, encumbered by their booty, were captured immediately. The rest spread out fanwise and disappeared into the landscape. The Sikh regiment turned out in pursuit and called for aircraft to provide close support.

The drama went on all day. Bombing of the Karesta and Bhittani was dropped, and the senior pilots all flew sorties in support of the Sikhs. Two aircraft were sent out to locate the attackers, but no sightings were made, even though shots were exchanged all the way up the mountain. A Pathan is more invisible from the air than he is from the ground; and on the ground he is hard to locate even when his bullets are kicking up dust beside you. On ambush, their traditional discipline was amazing. Lerwill told me that they carried hollow reeds to piss into, lest the sound of splashing water reveal their presences.

I didn't expect to fly on this important operation because I wasn't trained in army co-op. I hung about all day, fresh and rested and feeling left out. About 4.30 pm, however, Surplice called me into his office tent where Majumdar was also sitting.

"The army has asked for a last light sortie," he said. "I thought you'd like to do it. We've all flown several trips today. Everyone's tired. Shackels thinks you'd be OK with Corporal Stickland. You'll be taking over from Bill Traill."

Shackels nodded. "I'll give you a complete briefing."

When I arrived in the Latambar area I spotted Traill's plane overhead and we waggled our wings at one another. He turned at once towards Miramshah and the setting sun, and I took over the patrol. The hillside was swarming with Sikh troops, and a mile down the road was a collection of vehicles, including some armoured cars and light tanks. The pickets were still on the hill top and below them were medical teams getting their wounded down. They were not having an easy time of it on the precipitous terrain. When troops are advancing, wounded men can be left behind for the stretcher bearers to pick up. But when a withdrawal is in progress and the light is failing, the first priority is to get the wounded to safety. Long experience had taught the Pathans that if they applied pressure at this point they could pick up rifles and ammunition abandoned in haste. The Sikhs were not popular in Waziristan and a soldier who was left behind would be tortured with as much glee as if he were British.

I flew low over the ridge. It was 5.30 in the afternoon and the hillside was in shadow. It did not look as if the men high up could reach the road before dark. Halfway down to the road heavy machine gun sections were stationed, covering the withdrawal, their mules waiting patiently beside them. Some turbanned soldiers were still moving upwards, presumably part of the covering operation. Corporal Stickland had been three years on the frontier and had seen such situations before. He talked me round the unfamiliar scene.

"You won't see the Wazirs," he said. "They're miles from here now. That's my guess. Watch for the road down there. The Sikhs have got their HQ where those light tanks are. They may have some instructions for you. Always check first for messages from the ground."

I swooped over the road. A knot of officers stood in a circle, as if in a conference. Most of them wore turbans, but two were

An Audax picking up a message at Kohat, 1940. The message bag
hangs on a line between the two stripped poles and a hook hanging
from underneath the plane picks it up.

clearly British. I could see their round service hats and white faces. None of them waved at me as I passed over.

"If they've got instructions," Strickland shouted, "they'll put out a Popham Pamel."

"Thanks," I yelled back.

I'd been briefed by Shackels about the Popham Panel. It was a primitive device for communicating from the ground to the air. When the army needed air support they put out a large canvas square beside their headquarters. An M inside the square signalled that a message was to be picked up. Then two light poles were erected, joined by a wire from which a message pouch was suspended.

I couldn't circle in the narrow valley, so I climbed and turned and swooped down again, looking for a white square in the gloom, seeing nothing.

"There's no panel, Corporal," I said.

"They'll put it out when they don't need you any more, sir."

The light was leaking away as I crisscrossed the ridge, watching the machine guns being loaded on to the mules for the downward journey. An hour later they were almost down to the road. A few scampering turbans could be seen higher up, but the bulk of the regiment was lining the road and some had already entered their trucks.

"There's your Popham Panel!" Strickland shouted. "I can't see the poles yet."

In the deep shadow an M had been laid out and I descended with shut off engine towards it. Stickland kept up a running commentary.

"Left, left! Can you see the poles now? Get down lower. Lower. I've dropped the hook." All army co-op Audaxes were equipped with hooks which when dropped extended just below the level of the fixed undercarriage. "You still need to get down lower, sir. Otherwise you'll miss it."

I could see soldiers everywhere, many of them gathering round the poles, and I was fearful of taking off a head or two.

They seemed to have no apprehension of the danger.

"Lower, sir. Lower. That's fine."

We swooshed over the poles, and I was convinced that my wheels would tangle with the wire and take the whole contraption into the air.

"Message picked up. Perfect! Hook retracted and secure."

I opened up my throttle and climbed out of the shadow into the dark blue air and the setting sun.

"I'll read you out the message. Our thanks to Squadron Leader Jackson and all supporting personnel for help in our emergency. Withdrawal now complete. No further assistance needed. It's signed by the Brigade Major."

There was perhaps a half an hour of daylight left. The western side of the mountain was still lit by a red glow. I stayed until darkness obliterated the valley. It was very beautiful. I tracked the orange boards on the backs of the last picket as they reached the road. Then nothing. It was a black night of stars and the mountains gathered around me looked enormous as I flew the final time over the road.

Five oil lamp flares were laid out for me at Miramshah. Night flying was not encouraged here, because the Tochi pickets which climbed the neighbouring hill at dawn returned at nightfall, and the exterior of the fort was undefended. Six airmen ran my aircraft through the main gates and another team clanged them shut. Majumdar walked up while I still sat in the cockpit, his brown face anxious.

"Is everything all right?" he asked.

"They sent me home," I replied, "Corporal Stickland has the message."

Shackels read it. "Excellent. Excellent. Did you enjoy your first close support sortie?"

"It was wonderful," I said, rather stupidly. I could not describe my real feelings to Shackels. He was a professional soldier. He believed in army/air co-operation as an instrument of policy, as did the RAF professionals in 28 Squadron. I could only see the scene over Latambar as a gift, the fulfilment of a boyhood dream The pickets withdrawing down the shadowed hillside; the biplane, turning like an eagle in the dark blue sky, then diving into a cleft between the mountains. The Sikh regiment forming up on the road for the dangerous return journey to Bannu; the declining sun changing all the peaks of Waziristan to rose. It was many other things, of course. It was ambush and death for some. There was the fanatical bravery of the Afghans who had dared to challenge a regiment. But all I had felt was the beauty and the strangeness, and I could not express that to Majumdar. Fifty years later, the strangeness and the beauty is what I remember.

The bombing of the grazing areas went on, with less and less meaning, for most of January. I flew every day, and sometimes twice a day, and revelled in each minute, returning to Miramshah eager to try out my exquisitely timed sideslips and my fancy landings. They didn't always come off as planned, but one of the advantages of operating from a fort was that the flight office was inside the wall, and an ugly arrival was seldom observed. The 27 Squadron technician who had drawn the cartoon of me at Kohat had been transferred to 28 Squadron in the reshuffle and was at Miramshah to observe my new passion for army co-op. He drew another cartoon, showing me wavering in loyalty between a tank and an Audax. The caption ran—"How happy I'd be were t'other dear charmer away!"

Every evening the Political Agent delivered his panegyrics on the beauty and dignity of the wandering Wazirs, and I became convinced that the army—and therefore the air force—had no place in this wild and wonderful place.

"28,000 men," he would repeat, shaking his greying head. "What are 28,000 men doing here except to attract ambushes, kinappings and assassinations?"

The printing at the bottom reads,
How happy I'd be t'were other dear charmer away!
With apologies to one pilot (M-M?) or pilot?

On 20th January, while 31 Squadron's Valentias were still pounding away at the Shabi Khel, Major Duggal was brought in to the Tochi post at Sara Rogha unharmed. It was presumed, but never admitted, that the Indian government had come up with enough cash to satisfy the maliks. Major Cobb was cock-a-hoop with joy, having been right from the start.

> Diary entry: 23rd January 1940
> The report says that he looked well, but he is a nervous wreck. Like a shellshock case, they say. His wife had collected an enormous sum of money from sympathizers, on the assumption that the government would not pay the ransom for his release. She now has the problem of paying it all back to the contributors.

Later on Duggal's account of his captivity came to us through the intelligence pipelines.. It supported the common suspicion of the Khassadars, funded by the government but totally unreliable as a police force.

> Diary entry: 25th January 1940
> Duggal said that the bombing was not considered a great hardship. Most of them live in caves, anyway. The health of his captors (Duggal's report is filled with medical observations) was splendid. They never suffered from colds, in spite of their scanty clothing. They did not illtreat him, but they were extremely hostile to the British. One of them was an ex-trooper of the 16/5th Lancers. Not all of the maliks were sympathetic to the gang which had captured him, and they were shot at sometimes and had to move on to friendlier villages for food and water. The khassadars, however, were always disloyally supportive of the gang. No doubt they submitted a fictitious bill for ammunition expended in pursuit.

It is clear from my diary, its entries interspersed with verses, that the war had not fully entered my consciousness. I express a hope that it would all be over by next year. I was still dreaming of the walk across Asia that Ken and I had planned. The innocence of these lines, dated February 1940, makes that clear.

> Whatever's said I think we'll go again
> Once more together in the light of youth;
> And if we find our wanderings in vain
> Or blunder on the bitterness of truth,
> Peace and our homes will be more comfort then.
> We shall have known the best, completed wills;
> Ways white and winding, the desire of men,
> And paths that peter out amid the hills.

10

LAUGHTER AND
THE LOVE OF FRIENDS[1]
29th January 1940 to 6th June 1940

In the evening briefing on 29th January 1940, Majumdar told us that he was going to a conference at Razmak on the following morning and I volunteered to take him.

"Razmak ought to be shut down," the P.A. growled. "It performs no function and is a provocation to the tribes."

"It's an excellent training ground, sir," said Shackels politely.

"They could train anywhere else in the province. Why train in tribal territory and upset the maliks? The government's gone mad!"

Razmak was a fortress honoured in army circles. It stood at an altitude of 6,500 feet and was strategically placed at the junction of mountain trails that led from Afghanistan into the Bannu plain. Whenever there was trouble, Afghan warriors poured in from the north to reinforce their brothers and to profit by the

---

[1] From quiet homes and first beginnings
  Out to the undiscovered ends,
  There's nothing worth the wear of winning
  Save laughter and the love of friends.
            Hilaire Belloc

looting of rifles and ammunition on which their way of life depended. Razmak always had a garrison of at least a brigade to intercept this movement, but it was not particularly successful in its primary mission because there were too many alternative routes.

Its chief attraction for me was its notorious landing ground. There were, in fact, two rites of passage for junior pilots on the frontier. One was to fly under the Khushelgar bridge, and the other was to land at Razmak. The fortress sat uneasily on the slope of a mountain, its rows of ugly grey barracks contained by a low wall and protected by barbed wire obstacles and numerous searchlights. From a distance it looked more like a penitentiary than a military outpost. There was no level ground in the vicinity, so the military engineers had constructed a strip that ran directly up the natural slope. During the early Thirties all frontier squadrons flew the brakeless Wapiti. Landing uphill solved that vexing problem. I was flying an Audax with toe brakes, but there was still no way to land at Razmak except uphill, because the gradient was too steep.

On the way to Razmak the next day the ground rose steadily and snow covered everything, making the high fortified villages and the tracks joining them look like pencilled sketches on a sheet of white paper. The fall had not been great. Razmak was reporting an inch and a half which would not prohibit landing. On arrival I circled the base a few times, taking my time before attempting an approach. Shackels didn't try to hurry me up, appreciating that it was my first time.

Razmak was unattractive even with snow cloaking the scene, a blot on the majestic landscape. The parade ground was crowded with soldiers drilling. A contingent of turbanned warriors was approaching the north gate from a patrol. The landing strip was neatly delineated on the snowy surface and a staff car was parked by the windsock. This told me that my landing was going to be hampered by a stiff breeze, both crosswind and downwind; not the best conditions for a virgin touchdown. As I descended to a hundred feet the hill in front of me loomed threateningly and my speed over the surface was grossly augmented by the tailwind. Just before my wheels touched I had the weird feeling that I was slipping sideways and that my nose was pointed to the sky, and that no aircraft could land at such a tremendous speed. Then the port wing, which I had been holding down against the crosswind, stalled, jamming one wheel on to the ground. And so we skated along for a hundred yards with the port wing brushing the snow, until the other wing stalled and we were down on three points. Shackels, who could not have understood the complexities of landing crosswind, downwind and uphill, shouted "Well done!" through the Gosport tube.

After the conference I took off with all the conditions reversed—into wind, slightly crosswind and downhill. As soon as the throttle was opened the aircraft rushed forward, leaping into the air like a startled gazelle. I circled Razmak feeling very pleased with myself. Today it may be garrisoned by the army of Pakistan, carrying out the traditional task of keeping order in Waziristan. Or perhaps it is merely a historical site, the relic of an empire of the past, windows broken, looted beyond recognition, grass growing through cracks in the parade ground, the walls crumbling, the orderly rows of buildings falling back into the landscape which once saw the army of Alexander the Great marching into the Bannu plain. If an army is still there, my guess is that a helicopter pad has replaced the crazy uphill downhill landing ground I was so proud to have conquered.

A historian may be able to explain why 5 and 28 Squadrons went on with their daily attacks on the Shabi Khel after the return of Major Duggal. Major Cobb must have been right in thinking that the Indian government, having secretly bribed the maliks to release him, refused to acknowledge to their right hand what their left hand had done. My typical log book entry of the period was, "Destructive bombing Shabi Khel. 2x250 lb bombs." The Valentias of 31 Squadron continued to bomb up at Miramshah, attack the

Shabi Khel, and fly back to the safety of Kohat at night. I noted the names of the pilots—Ken Mackie, Dudley Burnside, Paddy O'Neill, B.W. McMillan. McMillan was a quiet sandy haired New Zealander who had already acquired a reputation as a pilot. After the War he joined B.O.A.C. (afterwards B.E.A.) and was captain of the ill-fated 'Star Tiger,' which disappeared tragically on the Far East route.

The cave in which Duggal had been imprisoned was identified high up on the range and it provided us with bombing practice. On January 27th I maneuvered around the mouth of this cave while Corporal Stickland took oblique photographs with a hand-held camera. It was the largest cave in the area and a low wall had been built across its width, giving the impression of a toothy grin.It was not far from the Karesta, and pilots involved in the proscription made attempts to lob bombs into the cave. I never managed this myself, but some lucky dive bombers knocked down most of the wall.

I volunteered for every flight available. On 17th February, for instance, I dropped mail on the main base at Bannu, then on to Biche Kaskai and Ghariom on the same mission. Later in the day I dropped a package on the Tochi post at Ladha, returning an hour later to drop more. In the evening I went to Datta Khel and Kar Kama posts, picking up outgoing mail by M.P.U. An exciting day, "flying low in the bright winter air, kept reasonably warm by an inner and outer flying suit, padded flying boots, and two layers of flying gloves." In those days we wore long silk debutante gloves under the padded leather 'outers,' and even then the cold got through to the bone. But I was in a flying heaven, conscious of the elegant lines of my Audax biplane, enjoying the rush of air in the open cockpit and the challenge of performing accurate maneuvers.

On 1st March 1940, a flight of 5 Squadron, the same unit we had bombed with flour bags and bog paper on Christmas Day, turned up at Miramshah for a spell of operations. The flight commander was Bertram 'Batts' Barthold, a lean quick-striding fellow, bristling with energy and professionalism. His friend and second in command was Michael Savage, tall and angular, with slightly absurd bodily movements which he was able to exaggerate for comic effect. He looked like an amiable flightless bird as he picked his way, with an abstracted smile, through life's obstacle course. His voice, over-precise, was that of a university lecturer. His father was the senior Mathematics master at Wellington College and a compiler of crosswords for the *Daily Telegraph*. We met in the mess on the night of their arrival.

Dinner was over and the officers were either slumped in the standard black leather armchairs or crowded round the coffee pots, always a favourite place to congregate and talk. RAF messes tend to be unnecessarily large, as if built in expectation of units that never arrive. In contrast, Miramshah mess was tiny and always seemed crawling with bodies. There was no fireplace to provide a focal point, so the obligatory reproduction of the monarch had been placed centrally on one wall with a long table beneath it. This was covered with six-month-old copies of the *Tatler* and *Punch* and more recent editions of *The Times of India*. It was cleared after dinner for the coffee ceremony. On the opposite wall was the library, a cabinet with glass doors stuffed to overflowing with books. Batts and Michael were standing in front of this piece of furniture.

"I've just decided," Michael said, "that Charles Morgan makes me sick."

He was suspending a copy of Morgan's *Sparkenbroke* by two fingers, as if it were a dead rat. Charles Morgan is little read nowadays, but in the Thirties he was a big name in Britain and the French literary establishment had turned him into a cult figure. He wrote mystical, patriotic, idealistic novels about sensitive souls who faced the existential issues with impeccable spirit. They

above: Michael Savage in front of his 5 Squadron Audax
at Miramshah, Summer 1940. *below*: An aerial view showing
the layout of the fort at Miramshah. Note the rows of tents
in the upper right.

flattered the reader into thinking he was privy to serious insights about the meaning of life. One of his pregnant phrases that had stuck in my mind was "the final ecstacy of death."

I got up at once from my chair and introduced myself. Michael introduced Batts. We had all read Charles Morgan.

"It's fake literature," Michael said, once again lifting the volume with a bony hand and rolling his eyes in beatific disdain. "It's milk chocolate for the masses." He was giving his famous imitation of the Mad Hatter in *Alice in Wonderland*, but for me it was a first performance. I collapsed with laughter. Finding that our incomprehensible mirth disturbed the other officers, we walked to Michael's cubbyhole of a bedroom to continue the conversation. There, with Michael stretched out on his bed and Batts and I on the floor, we composed a broadside to expel Charles Morgan from the canon of respected authors. It is necessary to explain that 'Mr Fry' appeared in all the current advertisements for Fry's chocolate.

> Charles Morgan thinks that love and verse
> And the last journey in a hearse,
> Will elevate the soul of man
> Higher than milk chocolate can.
> But we rely on Mr Fry,
> The flavour makes us swoon and sigh.
> It's always chocolate for us
> Who like the fun but not the fuss.
> Moreover we don't have to die
> To taste the final ecstacy.

We chanted this derisive silly verse in unison and were perfectly happy. Friendship is not as exciting as love, because there is no sexual element, but the happiness is as genuine. There was a stillness at the centre of our noisy laughter. I was being accepted into this group as a third brother. A younger brother indeed, because I was younger than either of them and not a professional

Cranwell product and because my romantic attitude towards flying was seen to be in need of correction.

Batts was not universally popular. He had a cheerful spirit of improvement, but little tact. One day while we were at Miramshah the aircraft were being bombed up outside the fort gates, and I walked out with him while he checked up on his flight. I can see him now. He had a quick long stride, with his head pushed slightly forward, giving him an eager look. In spite of his perfectionism there was an informality about him. He was often hatless and never looked particularly tidy. It was part of his sea-green incorruptibility, that he concentrated only on essentials. He was the opposite of the parade-smart dumb officer. On this morning the 28 Squadron aircraft were lined up close to the gates and the 5 Squadron kites were further out. It was a busy scene, with coolies in tribal dress pushing bomb trolleys and refuelling Bowsers into position, and technicians swarming round the aircraft doing their inspections. As we passed a 28 Squadron Audax he stopped abruptly.

"Look at that!"

"What?" I asked, seeing nothing unusual.

"That's the most dangerous procedure I've ever seen."

I wouldn't have seen a dangerous procedure if it blew up in my face but Batts was knowledgeable about virtually everything to do with flying. He knew about aircraft maintenance, could take a machine gun apart, adjust gunsights and a hundred things of which I was ignorant. He clearly knew about the routines for bombing up aircraft. He turned aside and spoke in a kindly manner to the armourer who had omitted some safety procedure. It took fifteen minutes. The bomb had to be removed from the rack and replaced on the trolley. A 28 Squadron NCO came up and Batts explained the regulation and what good sense it made to comply with it. He wasn't at all confrontational. It was do-gooding at its best.

At lunchtime Stott, my least favorite brother officer, called me over, his moustache bristling with hostility.

"That friend of yours in 5 Squadron is an interfering prick," he said, in his aggressive Yorkshire accent. "Wilf Surplice is filing a complaint against him. Barthold better mind his own bloody business."

In any event, the conflict came to nothing. Batts explained to Wilf that he was just trying to help out, and his version was accepted. But it was typical of Batts not to heed political issues. He went ahead with saintly confidence doing what he considered the right thing. In a world not governed by politics and smooth talking he would have risen to the highest rank in the Royal Air Force. But after the war there was an era of mediocrity and progressive disarmament which had no special need for his integrity.

It intrigues me to think how different we were. Batts so professional and me so determined to put romance and adventure before anything else. One evening, crowded into one or other of our tiny bedrooms, the question of my membership in 28 Squadron arose.

"They've been pretty decent to me," I said, "but I don't feel comfortable in an army co-op outfit. I'm not an Old Sarum man.[2] They put me on proscription bombing all the time because that's all I'm good for. I only get close support sorties when no one else is available."

"We must get Geoffrey into 5 Squadron," Batts said, looking at me affectionately.

"For training and improvement," added Michael, doing his mock tutorial Mock Turtle.

"And to amuse us."

"With his juvenile mind."

"Are you serious?" I asked, staring at them both and realizing that they were serious even as they laughed in my face.

---

[2] The School of Army Co-operation, Old Sarum, in Wiltshire is where Army Co-op pilots and army/air liaison officers are trained.

"Oh, yes," said Batts, monkey-like with glee. "We're going to be a fighter squadron in a few weeks time. That was a secret you didn't know. We're converting to Harts, and the first Hawker Hurricanes to reach India come to us. I'll ask for you specially, lying about all your excellent qualities. I know some people in Delhi. In a fighter squadron, we'll all be ignoramuses together."

Of all the acts of friendship I've received in my life this was the most surprising and the most significant. He was as good as his word. Directly they returned to Manzai he began wangling me a transfer to 5 Squadron

On 28th February, the Tochis were having trouble at Spinwam. A routine patrol establishing daytime pickets on the hilltop ran into gunfire and asked for help. I was not involved because I flew an early Ahmadzai sortie with an air gunner my own age called Lowry. We carried no bombs, but Lowry used his Lewis gun and I straffed with the single front gun which fired through the propeller, neatly arranged so that the rounds missed the turning blades. The area was perfect for split-arse flying,[3] empty of cattle and people, and I screeched around with my wingtip brushing the ground while Lowry pumped lead into an open barn door.

At lunchtime Shackels asked me to ferry him to Kohat for a conference.

"We can have a look at Spinwam, and there's some mail to be dropped on Thal," he said. Thal was an army post with a landing ground about thirty miles north east of Miramshah. It was the railhead of a line from Karachi through Kohat which at one time had been planned to run up the Tochi valley as far as Razmak and had been abandoned as being too vulnerable to tribal dynamiting.

Two miles from Spinwam we found an Audax cruising over a band of scrambling Tochis, obviously returning to the fort.

---

[3] Slang for crazy.

"That's Johnny Ironmonger," said Shackels. "The show is over."

I gained height to 6000 feet to pass over the high range and headed for Thal. A few minutes later the engine began to run rough, losing power and making a nasty banging noise. I throttled back.

"What's the matter?" Shackles sounded anxious. I was busy looking for an area to force land.

"Beats me."

I switched off the port magneto to test it and the engine cut out. I rapidly switched it on again. The country we were flying over belonged to the Ahmadzai, the very people we were currently bombing.

"We may have to force land, Shackels. We're five miles from Thal, though, and I can see the Kohat Plain."

"Wouldn't be much fun landing on the Ahmadzai," Shackels said. "They don't like us down there."

I could see Thal beyond the range of hills. If the engine failed completely I would not reach it. It was a fine evening, and every rock, bush and shadow showed up in extreme detail. There was nowhere to make a decent landing, though I could imagine an acceptable crash by knocking my wheels off on a rock wall and sliding to a stop on a level slab, risking being thrown down the next precipice if my speed was excessive. Then the people living in caves would run downhill, eager to cut us up into pieces slowly.

On my starboard wing was the Bannu Plain and comparative safety. But I didn't want to land in a field full of boulders and wreck my beautiful Audax, so I pressed on towards Thal, gradually losing height, my throttled back engine still giving some power. For a few minutes I held my breath as we brushed the mountain tops, and I knew that if the engine quit then we'd have to go down where no Tochi *gasht* headed by Loppy Lerwill could save us. Suddenly the mountains fell away and Thal was below me, deliciously reachable. At this point the engine made a loud noise and stopped, the prop rigid and crosswise to my line of sight. Shackels kept quiet as I descended. It was weird. The silence. Only the rush of air, the hiss of wires, the immobile propeller.

Thal had the standard square emergency landing ground and its windsock hung limp in the evening air. As I glided back and forth over its southern limits the view was dramatic. From Thal the ground rises steeply to the north and the Kurram River cuts a narrow passage as it rushes in from Afghanistan between high mountains, passing through Thal and Bannu before flowing quietly into the Indus at Lakki. The landing ground was perched on an escarpment beside the little town, overlooking the valley. It was just outside tribal territory and had a small garrison. I could see the railway line stretch out to the east towards Kohat sixty miles away.

I came in on a long steady sideslip, no fancy stuff if you have to make it at the first attempt; but I scared myself by cutting it too fine, forgetting that a throttled back engine is more efficient than a dead prop. I scraped in over the boundary by a hair and came to a stop by the concrete circle in the middle. Shackels bounded out and began to wave his arms in the air and shouting. In a minute three chowkidars, one with a rifle and bandolier over his shoulder, came running towards us. I had never heard Shackels speak Urdu before, only Harrovian English, and it turned him back into an Indian again, even his body movements altering.

"They'll push the aircraft to one corner," he said to me, effortlessly re-entering his Anglicized persona. "Get it out of the way in case someone else decides to land here. I know the army people here. They'll lend us a staff car to get to Kohat."

"Tell them not to refuel the kite," I said. "It may have to be lugged back for servicing."

I never found out what was wrong with the aeroplane. The technical people must have fixed it up because Audax K5571 appears in my log book later on. I flew back to Miramshah the next day in a back up aeroplane.

> Diary entry: 21st May 1940
>
> Lawrence of Arabia was at Miramshah for eight months in 1928, calling himself Aircraftsman Shaw. I've asked around, but no one remembers him. He'd written *The Mint* (unpublished), an account of his life in the RAF, and was busy translating *The Odyssey*, and working on the aircraft. He loved the isolation here and was sent home hurriedly because of an utterly false press rumour that "Colonel Lawrence" was involved in a plot to dethrone Amanullah, the ruler of Afghanistan!

When Batts and Michael left in April to return to Fort Sandeman, I was friendless once again. I didn't believe Batts could get me transferred from one squadron to another, but I was grateful that they wanted me. The idyllic few weeks had, however, made a profound change, and I felt for the first time at home in the Royal Air Force, instead of seeing myself as a mere short-service pilot, hopelessly inexperienced in flying, and lacking the right attitude. Reinforcement had also come from Majumdar, who made up for the camel incident by favouring me in whatever way he could. I was beginning to get the chip off my shoulder.

The Political Agent, Major Cobb, also began to take an interest in me. He was a bachelor and I felt sorry for him, locked up for long periods in a fort and twice the age of most other people at Miramshah. But he was the uncrowned king of Waziristan and I was flattered by his attention. He began to invite me up to his private quarters which overlooked a garden. I had not imagined that a garden could exist in such a place. He had more space to himself than the entire contingent of RAF officers, with their miniscule bedrooms and their inadequate mess. In the hot weather he wore a khaki bush jacket, voluminous shorts and

Argyle stockings. A small brown trilby hat completed the impression of some dotty Victorian explorer or butterfly catcher.

The dinners he asked me to were worth eating. He had his own cook, who appeared from time to time humbly enquiring whether all was well. His bearer was a handsome young Pathan, dressed immaculately and wearing a *pagri* showing the colours of the Tochi Scouts. They conversed rapidly in Pashtu, smiling and sometimes laughing together. I felt at times that I was part of the joke, but I couldn't be sure.

One evening I asked him about Persian poetry and he told me the story of the poet Hafiz, who had written the verse, "For the little mole on my lady's cheek I would give the cities of Bukhara and Samarkand." The Mongol prince, Timur, who had conquered India, objected to a pennyless poet disposing of cities that belonged to himself. Hafiz replied, "I am but dust and you are the shadow of God on earth, but it is owing to such misplaced extravagance that I have become the beggar that you see today."

"Of course, a lot of Persian poetry is rather naughty," he added.

"Naughty?"

"Well, it's about loving boys, you know. Quite naughty some of it." I couldn't find anything to say and he added, "Well, people don't always understand, dear boy."

In those days I was quite unconscious of the homosexual option. It never occurred to me that the P.A. might have found me sexually alluring. His "dear boy" meant nothing to me. It simply reminded me of the talk of actors backstage at provincial theatres in England. I remained puzzled by his friendship, but I was always interested in his talk and grateful for his kindnesses.

> Diary entry: 26th May 1940
> Tea and tennis in the P.A's garden this evening. Polite conversation in the atmosphere of a turkish bath. Major Cobb attentive to me. Showed me all round his

quarters and his neat well-ordered garden. The flowers and vegetables are separated by brick walks. Exotic creepers on the angle of the fort wall. He has an interrogatory style. "I used to have the roses over there, what? See how well they've done, eh? Don't you think so? Lettuce moved this year. Used to be over by the rabbit hutches. Too close to the rabbits, what?" Before dinner the P.A. had a small ceremony to present Frontier Medals to half a dozen Tochi Scouts. Loppy was there and some other officers. The sahibs sat in a row of chairs under a striped awning. A group of dancing boys from Bannu had been laid on as entertainment. They were half naked, and adorned with bangles and beads which jingled as they moved. Rouge and mascara on their brown faces. A Pathan with a stringed instrument and a foot drum made music The dancing was nothing if not sexual, and the conductor, a middle aged Pathan who carried a baton, made outrageous gestures with it which made everyone laugh. The P.A. was enjoying himself. "This is an excellent troupe, what?" he said. "Though I've seen better. We had a group from Peshawar a month ago, rather older boys and more experienced. This lot was very young, I thought." Major Cobb would really like to be a Pathan. He's given his life to the province and has learned to enjoy what they enjoy. After a shower I had dinner with him. Superior food. No wine. The talk was political. He told me that the most accomplished outlaw was Sher Ali, who made two successful attacks on the Royal Ulster Rifles. Gulfraz and Fezel Din were Afghan freebooters, posing as Robin Hoods, and not liked by the people here who can see through them easily enough. They embarrass the more sensible maliks, who stand to lose when the Afghans attack convoys in their territory. But everyone is terrified of them. Mir Dhil is the most dangerous outlaw because he has an axe to grind. He lost two sons, aged eleven and sixteen, in the bombing of the Sham Plain in 1937. He swears he will kill a British officer.

This was the last frontier entry in my journal. On 6th June a signal came assigning me to 5 Squadron which had been re-located at Lahore in the Punjab. Batts had made good his promise.

Miramshah remains encapsulated in my memory, like a dream from a different century. Its location was as remote as a Cistercian monastery, and it shared other elements with a religious house. There were no women. The outer gate clanged shut at sunset. The P.A. was as kind and strange as any abbot. The war against outlaws was a game which claimed fewer lives annually than the London-Brighton road. The flying was the best I've ever enjoyed. Much of it being close to the ground in wild country with the hills providing interest and danger; covering troops, picking up messages, scouting for road blocks in the steep defiles and dropping mail at the Tochi posts whose names will always be a part of my personal poetry. Ghariom, Bichi Kaskai, Datta Khel, Kar Kama, Ladha, Damdil, Spinwam, Sara Rogha.

11

FIGHTER BOY
9th June 1940 to 30th November 1940

Diary entry: 14th June 1940

Flew back to Kohat on 9th and took the train to Lahore on 12th. Welcome from Batts and Michael. Can't believe my luck! Batts is training everyone in fighter tactics from the latest fighter boy experience in England. We are to get Hurricanes as soon as they're available. The other pilots in "B" Flight are Willy Wilson, a weedy blond who looks as if he'll snap in half. Johnny Haile, another Cranwell boy, balding, a bit weird and solemn. Eric Cawdrey, a chain-smoking nervous type who they all address as "Ericses Cawdreys," as if he were in the plural. I don't know why.

Lahore is a great Mogul city. Akbar and Shah Jahan built the fort and Aurangzeb erected the huge 18th century Badshahi mosque. Just taking off from the grass airfield one sees these magnificences. Five miles south of the city, close to the British military cantonment, are the Shalimar Gardens, grander than the gardens on the Nagim Bagh in Kashmir. Rudyard Kipling's father was curator of the Lahore Museum, where all the Greco-Bhuddist sculpture is. In comparison to Kohat, the cantonment was enormous, but not as self enclosed. It was ruled by a triumvirate; the brigadier commanding the Lahore District Headquarters, the station commander of the Royal Air Force, and the senior Indian Civil Service official. Under them the officers of the garrison formed an aristocracy of knights and pages who could sally forth into the neighbouring city, clad in the armour of their rank and status, and throw their weight around. In those days the two major hotels were Nedou's and Falletti's. Batts and Michael used to dine in town once a week, and as soon as I arrived we all went together, ending up at the Metropole, a night club which provided some entertainment.

The comedians, dancers and singers could not have made a living in Europe. They were a species of wandering minstrel, acceptable to the far flung British because there was nothing else. Their only rivals were excruciating amateur theatricals. It was pathetic, but somehow heartwarming that these people had the courage to travel the world, poorly rewarded and not much appreciated. I had a fellow feeling for them. My cousin, Hugh French, magnificently goodlooking, had gone to the Royal Academy of Dramatic Art, along with Sexy Rexy Harrison, and they had both been chorus boys in early Noel Coward musicals. As a twelve year old I had been backstage, thrilled by the funny, kind, greasepainted actors and the half dressed girls. I knew firsthand (because I loved Hugh) the misery of waiting to be 'in work,' and I stayed with him in shabby 'digs' in provincial cities while he played in third-rate music halls. In Bradford one summer Louis Armstrong was top-of-the-bill, and I used to sit in his dressing room after each performance praising him, while he grumbled huskily about the band, about Coleman Hawkins (the great tenor sax) and his own terrible playing. The artistic temperament! Nothing was ever right with Louis, that kind and generous man. These fifth-rate acts that toured India and Singapore were in the same trade, but so far down scale as to be invisible. I bled for them.

After the show, dancing went on until one o'clock in the morning. Girls had been non-existent in Kohat, but Lahore was the headquarters of a military district and some of the senior officers had nubile daughters. It was at the Metropole that I first saw her. We were sitting on high stools at the bar and watching the dancers. She was with a tall man in a dinner jacket. He was fair haired and wore glasses She was very animated. A perfect smallish nose, chiselled by nature's most subtle art, and a big mouth. I learned afterwards that she was called 'Gobbie' at her boarding school, but as a grownup the contrast between the refinement of her nose and the sensuality of her mouth was a tour de force. I looked at Batts and gasped audibly.

"No chance there," said Batts. "They look engaged."

"They do," I replied, watching her laugh up into his glasses.

To my amazement I saw her again, surrounded by her family, at the Cantonment Catholic Church on Sunday. I managed to sit where I could watch her. After the Kashmir incident my morale regarding women was low. I didn't even fantasize that I could be in possession of such a creature. I was riding a Brough Superior motor bike I'd bought from Slim Olney, and as I pulled the heavy 120 mph monster off its stand I saw the whole family, three daughters and a younger boy, get into an old Chevrolet and drive off. Not one flicker of amorous ambition disturbed my mind. I had convinced myself that there was something screwy about me that put girls off. Anyway there were so few girls and so many chasing them. I wasn't likely to be a winner. Forget it. I had a slight advantage in being a Catholic, but it wasn't enough to give me hope.

> Diary entry: 28th June 1940
>   Batts is great. He cracks the whip and we all per-
> form for him like animals at a circus. Formation
> take-offs, battle climbs to 15,000 feet, loops in forma-
> tion (he won't risk our skills on a slow roll yet, thank

God) and today Michael and I bounced and rocked and titupped beside him as we landed, but Batts was quite pleased with us. He has good nerves!

Watched the girl in church again. Flowered summer dress, no stockings. Her father has red hair going grey and one of her sisters is a strawberry blonde. The girl herself has brown hair with just a tinge of red in it. The mouth belongs to another face, but I love it.

In July the heat in Lahore is oppressive. Batts kept us flying all day and I came out in a rash of prickly heat. The doctor gave me some powder to put on and I moved my bed into the garden and tried to sleep under a mosquito net, but it was no good. The noises of the Indian night kept me awake, and the temperature didn't cool off enough to make it worth while.

"You haven't had any rest for a year," Batts said to me one evening. I'd been showing him my powdered stomach that looked as if a cat had been using it as a scratch pad. "You've notched up five hundred hours on the frontier. You deserve a spell in the hills."

So I took leave on 16th August and met Patrick Biggie in Mussoorie, the nearest hill station to Lahore. Pat had been at school with me, one class ahead, and we did not meet until he was in his last year and head of the school. Our first encounter was in the hall under the big clock, where the headmaster took morning prayers. I was a prefect at the time and Pat tried to speak to me sensibly about one of my duties, but we ended up laughing uncontrollably at one another in the empty hall. I can see the afternoon sunlight coming through the stained glass windows and the reflections on the polished parquet floor and both of us doubled up in unseemly fashion. We were both trying to write poetry and exchanged derivative verses and our fantasies about women. Pat was in love with a girl who worked in the local library and he took me to view this paragon who neither of us dared to speak to, unless offering our library cards. His brother was a senior police officer in the United Provinces and Pat, after an interval of indecision, joined the Indian Police in the same ambivalent frame of mind in which George Orwell had gone to Burma.

The hotel we stayed in was full of old people. A few upper class Hindu girls who spoke English to one another glided through the public rooms, exquisite in their gold-trimmed saris. They would giggle like convent girls and then sweep out like fashion models on a runway, their faces expressionless. We were the only young males around and they put on a show for us.

"Look at their waists," Pat whispered. The sari is a graceful garment and shows the bare midriff to advantage. "But don't go on looking too long. Their parents have arrranged their marriages. They're just tormenting us." I would not be put off so easily. "They'll dance with us, surely," I said.

"Surely not," said Patrick.

> Diary entry: 17th August 1940, Mussoorie
> No English girls but some gorgeous Indian girls. At the *thé dansant* this afternoon I walked a mile of hotel lounge to ask the one we called the Queen of Asia, a real stunner, to dance with me. She smiled and was sweet and said no, without explanation. Then I had to walk a mile back, feeling rather foolish.

At breakfast the next day I suggested a walk, a trial by ordeal, an adventure. "Let us march across the mountains in a straight line," I said, "inviting peril and strange happenings." We studied the map in the hotel lobby. There was an old trail straight across the wilderness, joining Mussoorie to Chakrata.

"Chakrata is a tiny hill station," Pat said. "There may not even be a hotel to stay at."

"Perfect. There must be strict rules. We carry no food or water and take our chance of finding a lodging at the end of the

above: Patrick Biggie in the uniform of the Indian Police, 1939.
below: George Topliss at Risalpur, 1940.

day. Thus we'll leave ourselves open to encounters with giants, dwarfs and Paynims. Damsels in distress will litter our path."

"I can guarantee the Paynims," Pat said. "Everyone in this area is a Paynim!"

We set off after breakfast in our shorts and shirts and long stockings, leaving the rest of our stuff with the hotel porter. It turned out to be a track, not a road. In the previous century British families riding on horses, their belongings in bullock carts, would have made the journey of forty miles in three days. It ran steeply down for four thousand feet to the floor of a narrow valley, and then up again four thousand feet to Chakrata. There was no way of walking it in one day and we could see this an hour after leaving, as the way got steeper and the torrents swifter and the opposing mountain touched the sky.

Halfway down the jungle closed tightly round the path and the heat became oppressive. We came across a clearing in the trees, perhaps a natural phenomenon as there were no signs of human habitation. We threw off our clothes and plunged into the icy stream, drying off quickly in the strong sunlight. It must have been early afternoon when we reached the valley. Pat, who by this time knew how to speak Urdu, hailed a man who was working in a cornfield. In thirty minutes we were eating a meal of lentils that tasted better than anything a gourmet cook could produce from a royal kitchen.

The march uphill was hard going and we thought we might have to walk through the hours of darkness. However, as night fell we came across a *dak* bungalow, a goverment-funded resting place for travellers that may not have been in regular use for fifty years. The 19th century travellers, carrying their own bed linen and accompanied by their servants to cook and serve and fetch and carry, would have been very comfortable in such a place. We were not. There were no sheets or pillows or food or water or fans to make the heat more endurable. We dossed down on the bare *palangs* and continued our upward journey as soon as it became light. But we could not have been in a better mood. Chakrata, with its single small hotel, looked like heaven on earth. It sat on top of its world and was cool and attractive, and the proprietor was glad to see us as we were the only guests. We ate a huge lunch, washed down with pints of lager beer, and afterwards lay on our beds and talked till sleep came.

> Diary entry: 20th August 1940
>
> Pat's stories of life in the Indian Police are amazing. He was sent on his first job to a remote village where a tough guy had murdered a neighbour and was terrorizing the area. No one would talk and Pat's Sherlock Holmes act was getting him nowhere. A Police NCO, an older man, had been sent to advise him on this mission. After a few days he took Pat aside. "Look, Sahib," he said. "Everyone in the village knows who did the murder. Let me get a confession out of him." So Pat relented, with a bad conscience. (They did not teach strong arm tactics at the Police Academy.) Anyway, they beat the man until he owned up. Once he had been charged with the crime and was safely in custody, eye witnesses to the murder came up in scores to testify against him.

It struck me that Pat wasn't cut out to be a policeman. His interests were exclusively artistic. He had already begun to paint. He was a real expert on jazz. We had never before talked about anything except books and music. Brutality made him ill. He was a comfort-loving aesthete, yet he was involved with the most terrible of human activities. To make it worse most crimes went unsolved. Beating of suspects, and sometimes witnesses, often produced nothing but the victim's pain. The bride whose dowry had not been paid by her indigent relatives, was often disposed of by her husband pouring gasoline over her and setting her on fire. The perpetrators usually went free because the community was in a conspiracy against justice. It had been going on for countless centuries.[1]

On my return to Lahore the station adjutant summoned me and told me to report to Risalpur for a Command Navigation Course. I was up in arms. Navigation, for Pete's sake! What did I want with navigation? The subject stank of bombers, not fighters. They were trying to drag me back to 27 Squadron. I rushed over to Batts to express my fears. He picked up the telephone and spoke to his pal in Delhi.

"It's all right," he said later on. "They've set up a navigation school and they need students. You're not going back to bombers. Over my dead body. Johnny Haile's going too."

So I went.

Risalpur was 30 miles northeast of Kohat, close to the little town of Nowshera which sat on the banks of the Kabul River. For a decade it had been the home of the two other light bomber squadrons, 11 and 39. But by August 1940, they had been re-equipped with Blenheims and were employed elsewhere on coastal patrols. Risalpur was now half empty, its previously crowded airfield reduced to six Wapitis retired from 60 Squadron and one Valentia from 31 Squadron. I endured this diversion from my career as a fighter pilot with as much fortitude as I could muster. We sat in classrooms most of the day, and every other day flew in the back seat of Wapitis, setting course, estimating drift, working out windspeed and direction by observation of track and ground speed, and finally altering course to achieve our

---

[1] When the British government passed the Indian Independence Act on 15th August 1947, Patrick Biggie's career as a policeman was over. He joined the Diplomatic Service shortly afterwards and has served in Paris, Valencia, New York, Amsterdam, Athens, Barcelona, Havana, Seville, Kuwait and Johannesburg. In 1944 he married Peggy Barnes and they had six children. He retired and lived partly in France and partly in Chichester, England. Peggy died of a heart attack in 1998 and Pat joined her in 1999, also of heart trouble.

destination. In the hurricane-force winds of a rear cockpit it was no easy task to handle the map, the plotting board, the log and the manual computer all at the same time. Then peering out into the slipstream to establish a position by map reading. I often felt like throwing the map and log out of the cockpit and myself after them. The delightful thing about Risalpur was that George Topliss was there.

I had first met him on the train from Bombay in 1938, and we had already established a rapport. He was a tall person, large of limb, and possessed of a visage that could only be described as noble. He looked like a Trollopian Anglican dean, inevitably (on looks alone) to become a bishop.

One weekend we drove north in George's car to Tacht-i-Bhai a temple area on a remote hill where sat gigantic Buddhas with Grecian features, a heartrending reminder of the conquest of Alexander the Great. I had seen Greco-Buddhist sculpture in the museum at Lahore, but here it was displayed majestically in the open country, like Stonehenge. Bob Frogley, an ex-28 Squadron pilot and Angus Aberdeen, the station equipment officer, were with us and we sat eating our sandwiches in this idyllic spot.

"I don't approve of such delicacies as smoked salmon sandwiches," said George. "But I'll partake of some out of Christian fellowship."

George affected a high-minded spirit of self sacrifice which went with his appearance. The role of his friends was to reveal, under his obvious hypocrisy, the real selfish and slothful George. It was a hilarious act and has persisted as a stock joke into modern times. Actually he was not at all slothful. During this period he was becoming restless and dissatisfied at being an equipment officer and not a pilot. Most of his friends were pilots, and they were all preparing to do battle with the enemy, while he sat in an office shuffling papers. 1940 was the year of the Battle of Britain and Churchill's speeches of defiance. It was unfitting that he, who looked like a benevolent warlord, should avoid the front line. So he began to bombard the authorities with requests to be transferred to flying duties. His applications were received with respect but no enthusiasm. George was older than the rest of us, and combat flying was a young man's game. I can remember thinking that twenty-five was middle aged. George was then twenty seven and much more useful to the war effort as a senior equipment officer than as cannon fodder. But he persisted, and won his case. If he'd stayed where he was and fought his war at a desk he'd have ended up as an air commodore and no one would have thought the worse of him. As it is he threw away his secure career to risk his life in the front line. Reduced to the humble rank of pilot officer, he flew bombing missions over Germany and won a DFC. Good old George!

The big Valentia waffled and rolled through the night sky. Its storage bays had been turned into a classroom and each student had a desk, a plotting board, ruler, a manual and navigational computer. Pratap Chandra Lal, a young officer in the Indian Air Force Volunteer Reserve, was in charge. He went up and down the two lines of desks assisting each student, providing information and giving advice. Throughout the night he called us up into the observation bubble to take our star shot with the sextant. Then we would have to go back to our seats and work out the ground position from the navigational tables, in the same fashion as Captain James Cook in 1772 searched for Antarctica. In this exercise. I was handicapped by having to put on my glasses to see the stars, and the embarrassment of having to admit that I needed them. Pratap was kindness itself and he ended up taking the shot himself.

"Have you all worked out your position?" he asked, walking up the aisle and smiling at the workers. "If you give me your answers, I'll make an average of them and we'll see if we can agree on a ground position and then work out our windspeed and direction." He spoke English perfectly with the slightest of

Pratap Lal as the author knew him in November 1940 at Risalpur.

accents. Having despaired of my solution, I observed him as he moved around and saw that he had a clearly impossible task. Almost everyone needed his help, and Pratap was so conscientious that he would abandon no one, not even me.

"I'm a lost cause," I said, as he tried to sort out my disordered calculations. "Try somebody else."

Meanwhile, having flown a triangular track to Sialkot and Mianwali we were on our way back to the frontier and the Hindu Khush. Pratap worked steadily on, starshot after starshot. He was, of course, responsible for the navigation of the flight, but navigating by the consensus of twenty students, who were slowed up by their unfamiliarity with the techniques, was like running a ship on democratic principles. Suddenly the Valentia tilted as if it had been struck by a missile. Maps and computors and drawing boards crashed to the floor and several people fell out of their seats, for no one except the pilot was strapped in. Pratap struggled towards the front cockpit as the aircraft turned steeply 180 degrees and settled down on a new course.

A few minutes later he returned and told us, in delicious embarrassment, that we had violated the border with Afghanistan. 'Duggie' Holmes, the 31 Squadron pilot, was aware that we were nearing the Durand Line but when he saw the lights of a city below, he knew it was Jalalabad and took immediate action.[2]

---

[2] A less detailed account of this episode of violating the Afghan frontier appears in *My Years in the I.A.F.*, by Air Chief Marshal P.C. Lal. Lancer International, New Delhi, 1986.

Regarding the photograph of the India Command Navigation Course at Risalpur, October/November 1940, it may be worth noting that Micky Carmichael flew Hawker Hurricanes with No. 451 Squadron, Royal Australian Air Force, in the North African campaigns of 1941. He was captured leading an advance party to set up an airfield while General Rommel's tanks were inflitrating Allied lines. He was released at the fall of Bardia in January 1942. He was killed later in the war, but I do not know the details. B.W. McMillan became a captain for British Overseas Aircraft Corporation (B.O.A.C.) after the war ended and he perished on the 'Star Tiger' which disappeared without trace on one of the Pacific routes. Prithipal Singh was the son of the Maharajah of Jaipur. Mahinder Singh Verdi, an officer of the

This episode endeared me to Pratap and perhaps I sought him out in the mess. Or maybe he sought me out, it's hard to say. After dinner one night we were walking up and down in the mess garden, and he said, "Do you know Robert Frost?" I didn't and he quoted me these magical lines.

> The way a crow
> Shook down on me
> The dust of snow
> From a hemlock tree
> Has given my heart
> A change of mood
> And saved some part
> Of a day I rued.

He had been educated in India, in a school which followed the curriculum and spirit of the English public schools. His headmaster, he told me, was an Anglophile Bengali who had complete confidence in his mission to save them from themselves by a Western education. Pratap saw through the man's lack of sophistication, but he profited all his life by knowing what an educated Englishman knew. We had so much in common that we could have attended the same school.

His grandfather, Prakash Chand Lal, had been called to the bar from Lincoln's Inn and was a judge on the Allahabad High Court. His father, Basant Lal, spent his working life in the service of the Indian government. Pratap was an Anglophile from his toes up and I suspect that his major friendships were with Englishmen. He was also strongly nationalistic, his passion for India's honour took the form of intense irritation at his people when they did not

---

Indian Army seconded for service with the Indian Air Force, survived the war but did not stay with the peacetime air force. Bond, Manton and Dunn were to be reassigned to the Far East, flying Blenheims, and I fear they may have become involved with the hopeless defence of Singapore, like Billy Bowden.

come up to his high expectations for them. He was not at all blind to British faults and limitations and he took as much amusement in them as Englishmen commonly do in their own absurdities. But he wanted Indians to outgrow and overtake their conquerors.

"Where's the North Star?" he said, staring up into a sky that was full of stars. "Put on your glasses."

"I have no idea."

"That's the most important of the skymarks."

"'I am as constant as the northern star,'" I quoted. "Julius Caesar. It's a purely literary reference. I'd like to bet Shakespeare couldn't find the North Star, either."

"What about Orion?"

"Of course," I replied. "'Many a night from yonder ivied casement, ere I went to rest, did I look on great Orion sloping slowly to the west.' All you have to do is to look upwards and see if anything in the sky is sloping slowly towards the west. Tennyson's a sure guide in these matters."

"Idiot! You really don't know where it is?"

"Absolutely not."

"Celestial navigation depends on star recognition. I'll show you."

He did. We practised every night and I soon learned to find the North star, Orion with his belt, Sirius the bright shiner, Betelgeuse, the Pleiades and many others. There was a curious pattern in my friends. They were all trying to improve me, to make me more serious.

There were a number of newly commissioned Indians on the station, one of them the younger brother of a ruling Maharajah, who drove around in a Lagonda sports car. Most of them were non-flying and middle-aged, still waiting for their uniforms to be made. They hung about the mess like exotic birds. One night Carmichael, a loud-mouthed pilot from one of the frontier

The Navigation Course class members at Risalpur, October-December 1940. *Top row (l. to r.)*: PO Micky Carmichael, 28 Squadron; FO B.W. McMillan, 31 Squadron; unidentified; PO Prithipal Singh, Indian Air Force; FO Johnny Haile, 5 Squadron; FO Sid Cooper. *Seated (l. to r.):* PO Howard Dunn, 27 Squadron; unidentified; Lt. Mahinder Singh Verdi, Indian Air Force; unidentified; PO John Manton; "Little Steve" Stevens, 31 Squadron; the author; PO Fitzpatrick, 28 Squadron; PO Bond, 27 Squadron.

squadrons, decided to make fun of them. He was a large brute with a huge sandy moustache and a born comedian of the coarser sort.

Pratap and I came into the anteroom together from our star-gazing and moved instinctively towards the laughter coming from a group of officers standing in front of the fireplace. The Indians had collected rather self-consciously on the available leather arm-chairs at the opposite end of the room. One of them wore a royal blue turban and a long pink coat, buttoned high on the throat and reaching almost to his knees. His trousers were of the fitted Indian kind which showed his spindly legs to disadvantage. His perfume could be smelt across the room. He was older than the others, a rich merchant from Lahore who had responded to the emergency by volunteering to be an equipment officer. The others were slightly more soberly dressed but all appeared out of place in this Anglo-Saxon preserve.

"Look at those idiots in fancy dress," Carmichael was saying in a stage whisper, smiling broadly and twitching his moustaches. "They smell like Piccadilly whores, too. Bloody silly trousers. I saw them being drilled on the square today. Nearly fell off my bike! They waddled around like perishing peacocks."

He paused for his punch line, his blue eyes glaring at them above the abundance of facial hair.

"They'll be climbing the bloody chandeliers next!" he said loudly. Everyone laughed except the unfortunate Indians. Pratap laughed. I didn't laugh. I took Pratap's arm and moved him away.

"I'm sorry," I said. "You're bound to get some fools with no imagination. I hope you weren't too insulted."

"Well, he was funny," Pratap replied. "I couldn't help laugh-ing. Open prejudice is easier to put up with than the other kind."

"The other kind?"

"When a person doesn't even know he's prejudiced."

"Well," I said, "you'll soon be on your own."

"Absolutely we will. And you and I will be better friends for that."

We smiled at one another knowingly.

"Last lines of *Passage to India,*" I said. "Not yet!"

"Not quite yet," said Pratap, emphasizing the quite. "But sooner than anyone thinks. And then the Hindu, the Muslim and the Sikh will be seen as brothers, not divided by the necessities of British policy.

"End of quotation," I said.

We all believed that there was a British policy of divide and rule which deliberately exacerbated conflicts within the empire. It was the clever British way of unfairly imposing our will on subject peoples with a minimum of armed force. But in 1999, as I write this, it appears that we were wrong. The hostility between Hindus, Sikhs and Muslims burns on without us, and British rule in India can be seen as less than Machiavellian.

> Diary entry: 30th November 1940
>
> "You've got to do well on this course, Geoffrey," Pratap kept saying. "Wrong, I replied. "I want to scrape through. To be the least distinguished graduate. To be the forgotten man of course No. 1, India Command Navigation School!" But he wouldn't stand for that. Every evening he conducted a private seminar, hammering in what he considered the main points. I had to repeat the formulae for map projections until I had them by heart. On the last day, when each student addressed the class on some aspect of the curriculum, he called me out to speak on map projections. He'd planned the whole thing! All the senior staff were there to be amazed at my elegant grasp of the subject!

12

AT LONG LAST LOVE
1st December 1940 to 20th December 1940

I returned to Lahore on 1st December via the Frontier Mail. Batts' training program was going full blast. In his enthusiasm to master the art of fighter tactics he flew all day and studied all night. Michael and I were more interested in the civilized aspects of Lahore. We walked round the Old City, musing on the vagaries of history, and after dinner would drive to the local movie house with our military greatcoats draped over our dinner jackets. It is unpleasant to recall that the ground floor of the cinema was set aside for Indians and the non-commissioned British community. The officers and their ladies sat in the balcony on club chairs. Sometimes we'd go to the dancing places where we could watch the women, and on our return Batts would draw us into his room to explain his latest discoveries. We also got involved in raising funds for the war effort.

> Diary entry: 4th December 1940.
> Today Batts led "B" Flight over the city at five hundred feet, while airmen in the rear cockpits threw clusters of leaflets on the population. They were written in Urdu and English saying, THIS LEAFLET MIGHT HAVE BEEN A BOMB! DEFEND THE PUNJAB

This is a replica of the leaflets dropped over Lahore
by the author and his squadron.

BY HELPING TO BUY WAR PLANES. GIVE
WHAT YOU CAN AFFORD TODAY. We flew in from
the southwest, brushing the battlements of Akbar's citadel and the onion domes of the Pearl and Wazir Khan
mosques, right over the Mall and the big modern
hotels, and finally out to the Shalimar Gardens. We
could see a lot of scampering and waving as the leaflets fell like snow.

1940 was a year of crisis for Britain. While I was dropping
mail at the Tochi forts, the British army in France was being pushed
into the sea. When I was watching the dancing boys from Bannu
with Major Cobb, the lighters, barges and pleasure boats were
picking up soldiers on the beaches of Dunkirk under murderous
air attack ftom the Luftwaffe. In August, when I was happily
walking with Pat Biggie to Chakrata, the Battle of Britain was
being fought in cloudless skies over the southern coast of
England. Even as Batts led us over the city of Lahore dropping
leaflets, Mussolini was invading Greece.

I was aware of these events like distant music. Flying and
friendship were the important things to me. Only long after the
war was over did I absorb the details of the war's progress
and.understand its significance. Letters from my brothers and my
father troubled me more. Sometime in December my father wrote
guardedly to say that Ken and Peter were both destined for "overseas service." That could only mean the Middle East, because the
British, having been thrown out of France and Norway, had
nowhere else to fight. Much as I loved my life in Lahore with
5 Squadron, I could not stand the thought of my brothers going
into action before me. General Archibald Wavell had just defeated
the Italian army at Sidi Barrani and the local newspapers had banner headlines of his victory. I told Batts my feelings of frustration.

"Keep your hat on, Geoff," he said. "We'll soon be getting
Hurricanes, and my guess is we'll be in North Africa early next
year, if that's where the major battle is. We'll be there before your
brothers are."

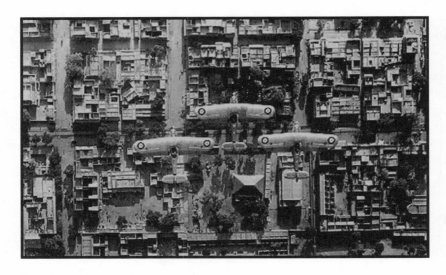

5 Squadron dropping leaflets over the city of Lahore, 1940.

*   *   *

The 15th December 1940 was a Sunday. Outside the cantonment church after mass I waited around to watch the girl leave. Her parents were bundling younger ones into a battered soft-top Chevrolet. I was about to steel myself to lifting the big bike off its stand—it had a 690cc J.A.P. engine and was formidably heavy—when one of her sisters, a red haired girl of about fourteen, pointed towards me. They all turned and looked in my direction. There should have been a roll of drums. As I stood there transfixed, one hand on the saddle of my machine, she walked quickly across the driveway towards me, her high heels crunching the gravel.

"You're back!" she said, touching me briefly on the chest, as if to assure herself that I was not an apparition. In a second she was gone and the Chevrolet had disappeared dustily up the road to the officers married quarters. I stayed where I was dumbfounded. Unsmiling. Grey-blue eyes. Plaid skirt. A black lace mantilla in her left hand. Solemnly she had looked into my eyes and touched me.

I mounted my bike and roared off to the mess. It was lunchtime. I didn't want a drink. Sat down but couldn't eat a morsel. Strode up and down the anteroom, smoking furiously.

"What's the matter?"

"Nothing."

"Sunday's a day of rest, old boy." Big joke. I walked out into the mess garden. I did not know her name.

I drove around the cantonment streets, looking at the large bungalows set back from the road. All had double driveways, verandahs with outside furniture, tidy lawns, flower beds. It was easy enough to read the names of occupants from the painted signs on wooden boards screwed to the massive gateposts. Major this. Colonel that. My fantasy had been that she'd be wandering the streets looking for her knight on his charger. She wasn't. It could not have occurred to her that I didn't know her name. I turned back to the parish church. Father Roger was bound to know the family, for cantonment parishes were tiny, Catholics

Joan at the picnic in Shalimar Gardens, Lahore, 1940.
This was shortly after we met.

being rare in the military. Most of the congregation was of mixed blood, progeny of the Irish regiments stationed in India because their loyalty was suspect, like the Connaught Rangers, who mutinied in 1916 and were disbanded. Ex-soldiers often took jobs on the railways and settled down with Indian wives.

Father Roger lived in apostolic poverty in a small building behind the chapel, part sacristy and part living quarters. I found him sitting in his office smoking a pipe. There was an easy chair for visitors, and a bookcase filled with spiritual works in French filled one wall. A faded reproduction of the Virgin Mary with a sword through her heart hung above it. He was a Belgian in his fifties, short and thickly built. With his beard and his Franciscan habit he looked fatherly and wise, a figure out of a history book. He had been counting the collection for the late mass. It didn't seem very much money. The missions, I supposed, were supported from Belgium. I got straight to the point.

"There's a pretty girl who sits on the left side of the church with her family."

"Ah, yes. Joan Lettington. I will write down the address for you." He had a strong foreign accent.

"Thank you, father."

"You will enjoy meeting them all. They are a fine family." He smiled pleasantly, waving his pipe and replacing it between his bearded lips.

A minute or two later I was parking my bike below the front verandah of the bungalow marked 'Major G.A. Lettington, R.E.' I could hear the shriek of girls' voices as I rang the bell. An Indian servant answered the door, but before I could give my name the girl herself ran into the hall, wearing a dressing gown and with a towel wrapped round her head.

"I'm Joan Lettington," she said, flashing me the widest and whitest of smiles. "And I know your name. You're Andy Baird."

We had dinner that night at Falletti's Hotel. The dining room was upstairs and we walked rather than take a lift. It was crowded with officers, their wives and girlfriends, but there were a few prosperous looking Indians in European clothes, their women in coloured saris. Waiters dressed in quasi-military uniform, with scarlet cummerbunds and huge white pagris, bustled about balancing trays expertly. I had never before taken a girl out and I was nervous about the wine and the ordering of dishes. I needn't have worried. Joan was bubbling to tell the story of our meeting from her point of view.

"Lots of officers have been leaving.the station. I thought you'd flown back to England and I'd lost you forever. I described you to people and they said your name was Andy Baird, and everyone said he'd gone home."

"He's much older than I am and has a ginger moustache."

"I loved that name. Andy Baird. You looked like an Andy Baird."

"You don't like my name?"

"No, I don't. Andy really suited you better." We both laughed.

"All my family knew I was interested in you. I nearly drove them mad with my Andy Bairdery!"

"I think you're wonderful."

"When I saw you in church again I thought my prayers had been answered. I just rushed across to you. I couldn't help myself. My mother says I'll come to a bad end."

We quickly drank the bottle of wine I'd ordered and I asked for another. The experience of being instantly approved by a beautiful woman was exhilarating and contrasted sharply with my previous dealings with the opposite sex. This was a convent girl, a year or so out of school uniform. I had a mental image of someone like her filing with others into the priory church, a swan among geese, unaware of my adoring gaze, crossing herself, kneeling down for a second with head bowed, and then sitting up on the long bench, her knees showing seductively below her gym slip. She was the fulfillment of my adolescent fantasies, grown tall, elegantly gowned, her face a compound of nobility and sensuality that must have been in my imagination from the beginning.

13

THE ART OF FLYING
28th December 1940 to 30th June 1941

December is the best of times in the northern plain of India. There is plenty of sunshine and the temperature is perfect for outdoor sports. It is pullover weather in the daytime and overcoat weather at night. I suppose there must have been rain at times, but my recollection is of bright sunlight, making the shapes of trees and buildings sharp and clear; and at night the stars seemed larger and closer than we see them in the West.

It was also the choicest of flying weather, the air always cool and steady. Our squadron commander was Dick Maling, a tall, spare New Zealander who looked not unlike Sir Edmund Hillary, the conqueror of Mount Everest. He had been a test pilot at Martlesham Heath and was known to be some kind of expert at flying. One Saturday morning he gave a personal display before the assembled squadron.

This was most unusual. Most senior pilots wouldn't stick their necks out. Who's this old fart, other pilots would say, trying to show us how to fly? Let's watch him make a fool of himself. The slightest error, the hint of a bounce on landing, would elicit jeers. When he'd finished his demonstration I was inclined to believe he was the best pilot who ever flew a plane.

He was basically a modest man, but great gifts will out. He was an artist, with that extra sensitivity that separated him from lesser mortals. A man who could feel the airflow breaking up on the leading edges of his wings five miles an hour above the stall. How could he have exhibited his talents farming sheep on some idyllic mountainside in New Zealand? In the management of horses? In the training of a pair of sheep dogs for the trials? In the air he seemed to be in control of the currents, smoothing the flow over his aerofoils like a bird. He made concrete the abstractions of thrust and drag, the counteracting energies of lift and gravity.

We all expected him to roar off and test the Hawker Hart to its limits. We expected to see tight loops and linked upward rolls, accompanied by the scream of wires and the blare of the Rolls Royce Kestrel engine at full bore.

"He's going to make this airframe beg for mercy," said Michael, genuflecting and spreading his thin arms in feigned supplication. "After this trip we'll have to ferry the kite to Drigh Road for dismantling and reduction to spare parts."

We were quite wrong. What Maling showed us was something more subtle and more difficult—aerobatics performed very slowly. He started out with a loop. A simple maneuver, one would think. But the way he did it was simple only in its perfection of line. It was so beautiful that I felt a shiver up the back of my neck, as if I were being moved by music or a poem.

He took off without any flourishes and climbed straight ahead, turning back to the airfield when he'd reached a couple of thousand feet. Then he dived towards us. At the beginning of the stunt I was puzzled, because he didn't seem to be flying fast enough to perform an aerobatic. We could barely hear his engine. He flew at ground level across the airfield, his wheels brushing the grass. Then, as he reached the tarmac in front of the hangars where we were standing, he climbed, changing his attitude with such delicacy that we didn't at once guess his intentions. There was no roar of engine power. He almost seemed to be gliding. As the nose reached the vertical I thought there was only one thing he could do—a stalled turn. But he was too low down for that. His flight path continued with perfectly judged momentum until he was on his back. He appeared to be almost hovering. There was a puff of white smoke at this point as his engine, being gravity fed, cut out. It looked deliberate; a grace note at the apex of the curve. Then, maintaining his arc, he flew round the rest of the loop, ending up at the same speed and with the same whisper of engine power. His wheels whisked inches above the identical portion of tarmac and the loop was complete. It was consciously aesthetic; a work of art carved ephemerally in space and time.

Afterwards he did a series of very slow rolls at low level before climbing up and performing routine aerobatics—rolls off the top, upward rolls—all at minimum speed and height. Watching him roll off the top of a loop, I was imagining the movements of his controls inside the cockpit. He was flying so slowly on his back that he must have pushed the stick almost fully forward to keep the nose up. Yet there wasn't a hint of difficulty showing, not a millimetre of nose drop as he hesitated before rolling out.

I had seen the Hawker Fury instructors at Hullavington give displays over the airfield, and had been thrilled by the snarl of the engines, the display of power and speed. Maling's aerobatics seemed to be directed at a different viewer, a lover of flying for its own sake, rather than the thrill-seeking general public. He was complimenting us by eliminating all the clichés.

His landing was typically understated. He dragged his machine in with a trickle of engine power, touching down, tail up, within feet of the boundary fence. Then he motored slowly towards the line of parked Harts, holding his tail up with throttle and checking the speed with toe brakes—a very tricky thing to pull off and one I'd never seen attempted. He 'walked' his aircraft in this tail up attitude round the control tower, turned neatly into

above: Batts *(l.)* and Michael in Lahore, Winter 1940-41.
below: Squadron Leader Dick Maling, O.C. 5 Squadron
flying a Hart aircraft. George Topliss is in the rear cockpit.

his original parking space, and stopped. For perhaps thirty seconds he held the tail up, before gradually reducing throttle and lowering it to the ground. We burst into spontaneous applause.

"I don't at all feel like following an act like that," Michael said. "The man's a genius."

Maling had arranged for the younger pilots to take off and show their paces directly his own performance was over. Batts Barthold and Bill Traill were to stay on the ground and do the judging. It was a horrible anti-climax. The aerobatics weren't so bad. We all did loops and rolls off the top and barrel rolls, but everyone bounced on landing. I tried to show off my swishtail landing and fell heavily on one wheel. This shot me skewed at an awkward angle into the air, and I had to open up my throttle to remedy the situation. We all received equal marks, which was rough justice. None of us was equal to the challenge after Dick Maling had shown us how to do it.

Joan and I went to the Metro that Saturday night. We were both wearing evening dress like people in a Noel Coward comedy. I was still using the well-worn dinner jacket my father bought for my sixteenth birthday. She wore a long black dress which I can't describe, except to say that it gave her a special dignity, and that it showed off her nipples.

When we were dancing it was clear that she was giving herself to me, innocently but seriously, as if she had been granted a revelation that the ordinary tactics of courtship were unnecessary. I suggested we go outside where it was cooler. There were french windows leading into the hotel garden and we opened them and walked through on to the lawn where a sundial stood whitely under a gibbous Indian moon. I kissed her. It was the first adult kiss of my life and it took a long time before we could speak.

"I love you," she said. I had not been expecting this. I laughed.

"But we've only just met."

"I love you," she repeated.

"The only thing I know," I said, "is that I must have you," finding inside my confusion a masculine capacity to take advantage of the situation. Looking back I am contemptuous of the young beggar, so magically transformed into a prince, who did not hesitate to use his mandate. Joan, however, was not hedging her bets.

"All right," she said breathlessly, looking at me with the slightest of smiles. "I'm ready."

The next weekend we drove off in her father's Chevrolet to Lahore.

I had booked a room in a downtown hotel called 'The Braganza,' run by a Goanese family. It was a cheap place in a side street close to the Indian end of the city, a mile away from the big hotels where I feared we might bump into people we knew. The brownskinned clerk who signed us in asked no questions, though we had lies prepared. He obviously knew what we were up to. It wasn't the best setting for first love. I began to wish myself back at the beginning, with the first kiss under the yellow moon and everything still in prospect. I signed us in as Mr and Mrs John Donne, having in mind those most seductive lines;

> So must pure lovers' souls descend
> T'affections and to faculties
> Else a great prince in prison lies.

I wasn't a pure lover, but neither was John Donne. He ended up as Dean of St Paul's. I, too, hoped to get to heaven.

The staircase was narrow and the little room contained only a bed and an oversized wardrobe. I wondered whether she would reject this drab place and I regretted that I'd not had the boldness to take her through the well-lit lobby of Falletti's and chance it. But Joan seemed not to have noticed her surroundings. As soon as the door was closed she shed her clothes on the floor and presented herself for the act of love. I had never seen a naked woman before and the effect of so much white flesh shook me.

She had done something similar before. I had been fiddling with her bra hook in the front seat of the car late one night. "Let me do it," she said, and with a vigorous movement she snapped the stitching that joined the two cups. That time I felt a surge of excitement and admiration for the directness of her sexuality. However this dramatic abandonment of all her clothing upset me. I wasn't expecting the challenge to be so sudden. The almost permanent erection I'd been carrying around ever since meeting her had disappeared.

It reminds me of the panic fear I had once felt when taking a public examination at school. For these occasions the gymnasium was stripped of its jumping horses, its parallel bars and the rows of hanging ropes that usually adorned the walls. Desks were set in orderly lines five feet apart. Prefects like Radziwill and Stephenson would walk slowly up and down the aisles to prevent cheating. I felt myself disintegrating. By the time the small printed sheets, headed 'Oxford and Cambridge Joint Board,' were distributed I was in such a state that I could not read the questions.

Joan was looking up at me from the bed. At emotional moments she would get a tear in each eye. It seemed to be under perfect control, in the way an actor can produce tears at will. She was not crying, but her eyes had this extra brightness. I sat down on the bed beside her.

"I'm sorry," I said. "I don't know anything about sex." This wasn't quite true. I had read that very misleading account of the sexual act contained in the unexpurgated edition of *Lady Chatterley's Lover*. So had Joan, for a dog-eared copy had circulated at her boarding school.

"We don't have to do anything," Joan said. "I love you. I just want you to hold me in your arms."

She was serious now. It made her look absurdly young and innocent, her clowning and sophistication eclipsed by this new intensity. I felt foolish and at the same time tender. I'd allowed myself to be intimidated by the plumbing aspect, whereas Joan had been thinking of love. Her tear-bright eyes could not have been lying. I had all the time in the world to prove myself. She loved me. The weight began to lift from my mind and the strength return to my body. I rose to my feet and took off my clothes.

At 2.30 am the next morning we drove back to the cantonment, married in the flesh and headed for a life together. For the history books, Joan's impulsive sexuality was never exercised on anyone else but me. She saved me, and saved herself, too, by the improvidence of her giving. I've never ceased to bless her for it.

We spent no more nights of love at the Braganza. We switched to Falletti's and braved the world. No one took the slightest notice. When we had first met she had been unofficially engaged to Sammy Moles, who was in the Indian Civil Service. She at once wrote to him breaking off the engagement but he would not accept dismissal. He turned up on the weekend after we had stayed at the Braganza to demand an explanation. The Lettingtons were hosting a picnic in the Mogul Gardens that Sunday afternoon and to my astonishment Sammy came along. I think Mrs Lettington still had hopes that he would outlast me in Joan's affections. The I.C.S. was more prestigious than the R.A.F. Sammy had a good post. But Joan was not hedging her bets and we wandered off on our own, returning only when the servants were packing up.

On 25th January 1940, Batts' flight took off for the bombing and air firing ranges at Karachi. We each stowed a suitcase in the rear cockpit of our Harts and took off like gentlemen in close formation, rising into the steady winter air like well behaved geese. We landed for refuelling at Khanpur on the Indus River where I had made a lonely arrival in August 1939. This time the three chowkidars took over two hours to pour petrol from cans into our five aircraft, though we all pitched in to help.

It was to be two weeks of intense flying, firing with our single front guns at target drogues. The ranges were off the coast south of RAF Drigh Road, the aircraft repair depot. It was a desert area dominated by the airship hangar, built for a craft that never arrived. When the 'Hindenberg' burst into flames while docking at Lakehurst, New Jersey, on 6th May 1937, the British airship program was cancelled. Afterwards the RAF put the hangar to partial use for aircraft repair and storage.

I suppose any kind of moving target practice is useful to the fighter pilot, but the Wapitis of the Towing Flight could only pull the drogues at 75 mph and the exercise bore little relationship to battle conditions we were likely to face in contemporary aircraft. But it was fun to be over the Indian Ocean in bright weather using our gunsights and our guns in earnest; and it was hilarious afterwards, counting the holes in the sleeves. Three aircraft attacked each sleeve, then it was dropped for inspection over the flights. The rounds we fired were painted blue, red and green, and ideally a bullet hole could be identified by a splash of colour and the pilot could claim it as his strike. It didn't work very well and half the holes had no paint on them. This lead to argument, protest and laughter. Batts tried to be serious about registering scores but Michael and I were too much for him. We made a farce of it and in the end he joined us. But it was good shooting practice even if we couldn't establish a winner.

The Wapitis towed the sleeves a mile from the shore at 4000 feet. We flew in the opposite direction and 500 feet above on the landward side so that when we turned to attack, the rounds fell out to sea. I scared myself on the first pass, staring down the gunsight, positioning the crossbar well ahead of the target, pressing the trigger on the stick (always called 'the tit'), hearing the crackle of the gun. In my excitement I almost ran into the drogue. It was probably my best attack because later I became too conscious of the rapid approach speed and the very visible and dangerous-looking towing line.

When my turn came to fly into action against the enemy, I flew fighters in the low level reconnaissance role, so I never shot down an aircraft, though I've had one or two opportunities. This

Hans-Joachim Marseille, the German pilot hero
wearing the Iron Cross.

frustration has led me to ask top scoring fighter boys what they really did to achieve their victories. What I discovered didn't have much reference to what went on above the pristine yellow beaches of Karachi.

Ray Harries,[1] who had more than twenty victories in the skies over southern England, shared an office with me in the Air Ministry, Whitehall, in 1946. A small vibrant individual with a great sense of humour and the best honky tonk barroom pianist I've ever heard, he explained his technique in this way. "I don't do anything fancy," he said. "I just get behind the Hun aircraft and close in until I think my prop will chew his tail off. Then I press the tit and fly through the bits."

My other authority is Peter Wykeham,[2] who made his name in the Western Desert in 1941 during the gallant and futile attempt to operate No. 73 Squadron from the Tobruk main airfield while it was under seige by the German and Italian armies. He stayed with me while I was in Gibraltar commanding 224 Squadron. It was in November 1950, and he had been flying around RAF bases giving his lecture on low level interdiction tactics. By the end of World War II he was an acknowledged expert. At the outset of the Korean War the Americans enlisted his help in training their operational crews. He was a big handsome blond Viking married to the daughter of the novelist J.B. Priestley. He was a writer, an intellectual, with a war record matched by very few pilots. He was also a superb lecturer. I remember how vividly he expressed his admiration for the U.S.A.F. crews he flew with in Korea, their spirit, humour and democratic manners. He arrived flying his own De Havilland Mosquito, and I was put in charge of his reception and entertainment. We stayed up late in my room talking.

---

[1] I am advised that the 1995 edition of Christopher Shores' *Aces High* revises downward Ray's total of kills, because of new research on shared kills, probables and damaged. I can't see Ray caring much!

[2] Air Marshal Sir Peter Wykeham, KCB, DSO, OBE, DFC, AFC.

I told him my Ray Harries story and he said, "Ray is quite right. Fancy stuff doesn't work for most people. But you know, there are exceptions. 'Screwball' Buerling[3] was a natural deflection shooter. He could see the exact point in the sky that his target would pass through and could attack at classic range, as if he were firing at a drogue. But I can't think of anyone else in that class." In 1950 I knew nothing of Hans-Joachim Marseille, the Luftwaffe ace—a deflection shooter with 158 victories—to put beside Buerling. On 14th September 1941, he had shot down my flight commander, Pat Byers, who was severely burned getting out of his cockpit. Marseille then flew twice at low level and at minimum speed through the murderous fire of our airfield defences to drop messeages. The first time to regret Pat's burning. The second time to regret his death from burns. Marseille was more than a superb deflection shooter, he was a very gallant and noble young man. I have tried to get this episode (described fully in *Messerschmitt Roulette*) to the attention of German military publishers, but without success. This is my second attempt to honor him as he he should be honored.[4]

By good luck Pratap Lal was also at Karachi. He had left his position as an instructor at the Navigation School and was doing a temporary job at Drigh Road before setting off for Ambala and his pilot training. I came with him into the dining room on the night of our arrival and introduced him to Batts and Michael. Michael was in a teasing mood.

---

[3] George 'Screwball' Buerling, a Canadian pilot in the Royal Air Force, made his reputation defending the island of Malta in August 1942, while flying Spitfires. He shot down a total of 33.3 aircraft during his career, making him one of the top-scoring British aces. He lost his life in 1948 ferrying aircraft to Israel.

[4] My article, "Lufwaffe Ace's Act of Chivalry," was published in *World War II*, a Primedia Enthusiast Publication in January 1999. I sincerely hope that German publications will take it up. If they do it will significantly strengthen Marseille's reputation.

Batts and Geoffrey worshipping the sand woman, Karachi 1941.

Brother Ken back from
Greece to join the Army,
October 1939.

"Geoffrey has found himself a woman, but we are still womanless," he announced. "It has put him into a superior category of human beings. He has outsoared the shadow of our night. We might as well be on a desert island."

"You ought to try being an Indian," Pratap observed. "Your problem pales in comparison with mine."

"Tell us about it," Batts said.

"As you see, Geoffrey could meet socially with a girl and find a wife, if he wants one. When I came back to Delhi after a year or two in London I had some fantasy of offering myself to some attractive Indian girl, and that she might accept me in the Western way of doing things. All I got for my trouble was blank incomprehension, or a confession that her family had arranged her marriage some years previously."

"Up at Mussoorie," I said, "I asked the most gorgeous Indian girl to dance with me. Nothing beyond that. I wasn't asking lewdly for a kiss or anything like that. She was displaying herself in the ballroom, so why wouldn't she dance with me, Pratap?"

"Apart from the fact that it would not be conventional, she was probably betrothed already to someone she may not have met. I have just made a big decision for myself. I am waiting in hope no longer. This very week I am writing to my father asking him to find me a suitable wife. I'm tired of living alone. My requirements, I will tell him, are that she should be good looking, well educated, and share at least one language with me."

On the weekend we all went picnicking on the deserted beaches of the bombing range. It was too cool to swim but fine for sunbathing. We talked the day through in a ceremony of friendship. Batts made an oversized sand sculpture of a woman with impressive thighs and breasts. It was a symbol of the sexual frustration of everyone except me. I still possess a photograph of Batts and myself worshipping this idol.

*   *   *

The plains get too hot for comfort as early as April and families begin to depart for nearby hill stations. Joan and I were parted when the Lahore District Headquarters, where she worked as a clerk, moved for the summer to Dalhousie in the Himalayas. We wrote to one another almost daily. She often signed her letters with the lipstick impression of her mouth to remind me of the pleasures at her command. I had never mentioned marriage. One reason was my pact with Ken to walk round the world. It sounds absurd in the light of history, but I still thought of the war as a brief interlude which might be all over before I had fired a shot. There was no war in the Far East and 5 Squadron's re-equipment with Hurricanes had been delayed. To summarize a muddled mind, I wanted to join a fighting squadron, distinguish myself in some way, walk with Ken across Asia, and finally marry Joan. It was pure fantasy, and part of me knew that the war was so majestic an event that it was going to absorb what was left of my youth; that I would never travel the world with Ken; and that even survival for England was in doubt. Joan, however, had her own agenda.

A telephone call from Dalhousie woke me to reality. I was Duty Pilot and alone in the airfield control tower after flying was over for the day. Joan's voice was faint but clear.

"Before you decide to come here for your leave," she said, "I want you to know that I'm engaged to be married."

"You can't be engaged! Who to?"

"His name is Roger Bateson and he's in the Durham Light Infantry."

"How can you marry someone else when you love me?"

"I do love you but you don't want to marry me. He does.

"Oh, for God's sake! I'll come up to Dalhousie to see you."

The next morning I begged a few days leave and was granted it. Dalhousie was the nearest hill station to Lahore and I set off on my motor bike early, thinking I would be there by midday and surprise her. Just beyond Amritsar the motor seized solid. Luckily

I was a mile from a village, though it was no joke.pushing the heavy machine on the potholed, dusty road, and passed by insolent camels and Indian families in *tongas*. During the two-hour wait for a bus I telegraphed Joan to meet me at the bus stop at Dalhousie. I was worried about her impulsiveness. She had declared herself to me without any thought of the consequences. She was quite capable of running off with Roger Bateson on impulse. One night when we had wanted to make love but had not booked an hotel, she came to my room in the officers mess. It was a gross risk, for officers quarters were not designed for clandestine entry or exit; but the adventure seemed to add to her zest. I knew she loved me. I must have missed, or perhaps stupidly ignored, her hints that she was not going to wait for me till the war was over.

She was standing there when the bus pulled in, her flowered dress vibrating in the wind against a display of feminine hip. We walked up the steep hill to Stiffle's hotel, where she had a room for the summer months. I knew then that this was a game and that she would marry me.

"Of course we'll get married," I said, my arm around her shoulder.

"Roger is a nice boy and very serious about me."

"We're already married," I said.

We spent the afternoon getting married over and over, and at six o'clock that evening we made our way to the Dalhousie officers club to explain the whole mess to Roger. I apologized as humbly as I could manage. When Joan gave him back his ring, he was moved to tears. He was a fellow of my own age and very much the regular army officer. He shook my hand.

"The best man wins, old chap," he said. He was probably the last man ever to mouth that Victorian cliché.

We did not set a date for our wedding. Joan had made her point and was pressing no further.

"I've got to fight the war first," I said.

She hesitated a moment looking intently into my eyes.
"I know."

When I returned to Lahore a letter from Ken awaited me.

> Diary entry: 29th April 1941
> Ken is in the Middle East. His language is curiously
> convoluted. I suppose to fool the officer who censors
> outgoing mail. But he makes it clear that Hugh has
> already arrived in Cairo and that Peter and his tank
> regiment are expected soon. "Hoping to see you soon,"
> he writes. Which is as near a direct order an older
> brother can issue.

I went to Batts for the final time and told him I must go.
"My brothers are in Egypt or soon will be," I said. "I just
have to fight the war now. I can't stay here on a sort of protracted
holiday while they do their stuff."
"What about Joan?" he asked.
"I'll come back to Joan. I have to fight now. I can't stay here
any longer." Batts was very sweet and put his arm about my shoulder protectively.
"I know, Geoff," he said. He was my substitute older brother.
He didn't take my separation from 5 Squadron personally. The
next day he picked up the telephone and offered my services to
the Middle East Air Force. My posting didn't come through until
June, but I knew I was going and was elated, in a fatalistic way, at
the prospect.

On 20th May 1941, 1 took off on a meteorological climb to
15,000 feet. It was a routine flight, with an airman in the rear
cockpit noting barometer readings every thousand feet. I climbed
in a wide spiral, enjoying the sight of the ancient city beside the
Ravi River, with its battlements and palaces and mosques. To the
east, as I reached 10,000 feet, I could see the glitter of Amritsar's

jewelled temples. About fifteen miles south of the city the engine failed. Down below me were the flat brown fields of the Punjab, offering a wide choice for landing safely. I picked out a square field that stretched along the dead straight road that ran from Lahore to Ferozepore. The aircraft would have to be lifted on to a transporter. It would be convenient for the technical people if I landed close to the road.

The day was perfect, not a cloud in the sky. I had done this trick before and I wasn't nervous at the idea of doing it again. It was pleasant, gliding without the engine, and I had twelve thousand feet of leisurely descent ahead of me. Out of a minor disaster I could make a work of art. Eighteen months of hard flying had done a lot for my self confidence. During the first weeks at Kohat I remember envying Logger Powley, the Canadian, for having 600 hours of pilot time in his log book. I now had over 600 hours in mine. By wartime standards that made me an experienced pilot. That was why Middle East Headquarters had jumped at my offer to join them. I was ready to face more formidable enemies than a dead prop.

Let us leave him there, in the blue air.

A few weeks later, on 5th July 1941, he will take off from the still waters of Karachi harbour in a Sunderland flying boat, stopping at Basra and the Dead Sea before landing on the Nile at last light. The next eight months were to provide him with the central challenge of his life. He would return to Lahore to fulfill his promises to Joan, but he would never again be the same innocent who slipped over the low line of trees that day to touch down neatly beside the road to Ferozapore.

AFTERWORD

Group photograph of No 451 Squadron, RAAF, November 1941.
Top row (l. to r.): Dave Strachan, RAF pilot; Bill Buckland, RAAF
Cyphers; Ron Achilles, RAAF pilot; Pete Campbell, SAAF pilot;
Harry Rowlands, RAAF pilot. *Middle row (l. to r.)*: Jim London,
captain, Australian Army, A.L.O.; Colin Robertson, RAAF pilot; Stan
Reid, RAAF medical officer; Kevin Springbett, RAAF pilot; Temple
Haddon, SAAF pilot; Spindle Ferguson, RAAF pilot; 'Acker' Kerr,
RAF engineering officer; Ken Watts, RAAF pilot; 'Blue' Thyer,
RAAF Cyphers; Morgan Bartlett, RAAF pilot; Ray Goldberg, RAAF
pilot; 'Mac,' RAF pilot; Bill Landslow, RAAF Adjutant; F/L Evans,
RAF engineering officer. *Bottom row (l. to r.)*: Micky Miller, RAAF
equipment officer; Ray Hudson, RAAF pilot; Ed Kirkham, RAAF
pilot; Paddy Hutley, RAAF pilot; Murray Gardiner, SAAF pilot;
Squadron Leader R.D. 'Wizard' Williams, RAF, Officer Command-
ing; Geoff Morley-Mower, RAF pilot; Chris Miller, RAF pilot; Hugh
Walford, RAF pilot; Charlie Edmondson, RAAF pilot.

Molly Malone, Pat Byers and Mickey Carmichael were already
either dead or injured, thus missing for the photograph.

14

FEAR IN STRANGE PLACES

Michael Savage was a prolific poet and he sent me this poem sometime in 1943. It was considered good enough to be published in a wartime anthology in 1944. The opening passage has stayed in my mind since I first read it.

Fear may come to us in strange places
As a face known but in a different environment,
Out of context, irrelevant, unjustifiable,
Childhood's nanny in the sailor's tavern.

Not always with the whistle in the slashed night,
Nor in the flooding hull, the flaming cockpit;
Even in the cold words of judge or surgeon
He may fail to keep his appointment.

Energy, apathy, bewilderment or laughter
May pay us a call in his place, but fear
Is the reveller coming to the dance at midday,
The visitor dropping in to lunch at daybreak.

Ludwig Wittgenstein pointed out that death is not "an event in life"; but the experience of being confronted by death is.

Knowing that every case is singular, I offer up my twopennyworth of wisdom.

I joined No. 451 Squadron, Royal Australian Air Force, in July 1941. It was a Hawker Hurricane fighter reconnaissance squadron. On my very first sortie in North Africa I lost my nerve in a box barrage. 'Molly' Malone, my flight commander, was leading this intrusion into enemy territory and he had chosen to fly directly over Halfaya Pass—better known as Hellfire Pass—a heavily defended German position near the Libyan frontier. It was a cloudless day, with the blue Mediterranean decorating the harsh coastline with a fringe of white surf. My job was to cover Molly's tail for enemy fighters while he carried out the reconnaissance, but we seemed alone in the empty sky at that point. Suddenly we were engulfed by a storm of black puffs. They were above, below, in front and behind us. The barrage had been set up to provide a well-organized package of explosions at a calculated height, and they'd worked out our height pretty accurately. Every shell burst was marked by a little black cloud and there were so many of them that inside the box it was almost dark. Tiny shell fragments drummed on the taut skin of my fuselage as we were rocked and juddered by the explosions.

Molly ploughed through this dangerous murk without taking any evasive action. I thought at any moment one of us was going to collide with one of those explosions and that it was probably going to be me. I couldn't stand it a second longer. I turned my Hurricane on to its back and barrelled down to the desert floor. As I flashed across the coastal escarpment at high speed, German soldiers ran wildly for their machine gun positions in a hopeless attempt to fire at me. Looking up I could see Molly's aircraft crawling out of the ragged, wind-torn barrage into the safety of the surrounding blue. Stricken with remorse, I climbed at full throttle to rejoin him, wondering if my desertion would be considered a military disgrace. It was a poor way to begin my operational career. Back at our landing strip—simply a patch of desert cleared of scrub and stones by the Royal Engineers—I walked behind Molly as he humped his parachute to the flight tent. I was expecting a cutting rebuke or perhaps the threat of a court martial, but Molly was only interested in teaching me the techniques of reconnaissance. He showed me his knee pad, covered with neatly inscribed data on the Halfaya position. "In this job," he said, smiling at me benevolently, "you must learn to write legibly, while at the same flying the aircraft." I nearly fell over with relief. Clearly he had not seen my desperate dive to safety. The visual confusion of the barrage would have accounted for that. Lucky as I felt at my shame not being discovered, it remained in my mind as a huge and indelible failure. Afterwards I made two critical decisions. The first was never to fly with madcap Molly again. The second was more important—never to permit myself to flinch beneath the axe as it flashed down on my unprotected neck!

Molly disappeared forever a few weeks later. He took to circling German and Italian camps at between 500 and 1000 feet above the ground, making himself vulnerable to both light flak and small arms fire. Charles Edmondson, the Australian who covered him on his last flight, described Molly's aircraft receiving a direct hit. "An orange flash as his petrol tanks went off, then his left wing dropped and he crashed into the ground on a diving turn. It was like a bomb going off."[1]

During the next eight months I must have spent a total of several days flying through light and heavy anti-aircraft fire. One of our jobs was taking line overlap photographs of the forward areas. It meant flying straight and level for an hour at 6000 feet, completely at the mercy of the German 88 millimetre guns. I loathed the feeling of helplessness it gave me. The more accurately I flew for the three downward facing cameras—unwavering course, steady speed and constant height—the easier for

---

[1] Charles Edmondson won a DSO leading an RAF squadron of the Balkan Air Force in 1945. He lives in Sydney, Australia, and is president of the 451 Squadron Association.

the guns on the ground to destroy me. But I volunteered for these revolting assignments because they forced me to be unflinching. It was a way of facing what I most feared. And it was just retribution for my mortal sin over Hellfire Pass.

Attacks by Messerschmitts should have been more frightening, but they were not. I was once cornered by two ME's just outside Tobruk, which was being held by the Australians. Happily I was close to the ground, and it is very difficult to shoot a plane down when it is in a steep evasive turn at low level. They played with me awhile, trying to turn me away from the safety of the Tobruk perimeter. I was elated rather than scared, like a trapped animal. If you asked an antelope how he felt when being chased by a lion, he'd probably say, "I'm busy. Not frightened. Just busy." I can remember the sweat falling down my face, threatening to mist up my glasses, as I raced in a circle, my wings vertical a few feet above the sand. But trying to fly accurately took all my presence of mind. The occasion was more like a game, hot and sweaty and too fast for thought. The outcome may well have been death, but the structure of the event was exciting and required maximum concentration. I was seated in a maneuverable fighter aircraft and aware of eight .303 machine guns in my wings. They could fight back. I knew also that the wing loading of the Hawker Hurricane was lower than the Messerschmitt 109. If anyone was going to flip over in a high speed stall and burn up on the desert floor it wasn't going to be me. I had forty minutes of fuel left in my tanks and I was prepared to stay in that steep turn for thirty-five of those minutes before making a dangerous break for the Tobruk perimeter. I didn't have to. They gave up after ten minutes of threatening passes that came to nothing. Shortage of fuel, probably.

Fear on the ground is different.

In October 1941, I was inside the fortress of Tobruk with my Hurricane stashed in an underground hangar. It was one of those secrets of the war that stayed a secret from the enemy. Before each sortie, General Morshead, the commander of the garrison, would brief me personally in his headquarters cut into the red cliffs behind the harbour. When I landed back from my reconnaissances, the airmen would rush my aircraft down a steep slope at the end of the landing strip and then push me under a camouflage net. Messerschmitts from nearby airfields would take off to intercept the intruder, but they never conned on to the idea that a Hurricane existed *within* the perimeter. We'd see them roaring out to sea, chasing nothing.

Tobruk was a weird environment. Bombardment went on all day from the heavy German and Italian seige artillery, and dive bombing Stukas turned up to attack specific targets. On my arrival I was issued a bivouac tent and a spade and told to dig myself in by nightfall. Everyone lived six feet underground in Tobruk. But by this time I had developed a fairly full-blown fatalistic philosophy. I argued that I was destined to die in the air and had no business being scared out of my wits on mother earth. Digging in made sense for soldiers but not for me. So I never used the spade provided. I planted my tent on the stony surface of the desert and was pleased to think of myself not only as the single airman in the fortress but the only person sleeping above ground. I refused to wear the conventional tin hat and hung it over one of the tent pegs. There it remained until I left Tobruk three weeks later.

When *Messerschmitt Roulette* was published, Charles Edmondson wrote to me about an incident I had forgotten. Tobruk had been relieved during the British offensive of November 1941, and our squadron flew in to occupy the main airfield. The military situation was mixed. Some German and Italian seige guns were still pounding away at the fortress. You could hear the dull sound, like a grunt, when they were fired; a pause as the shell ascended to its maximum height, and then the shrill scream of its descent. When the scream was highly pitched, immediately followed by a loud bang and the shaking of the earth, you knew it had been close. Charles remembers that we were eating in the mess tent

above: 451 Squadron Hurricanes on the tarmac at Rayak, Syria in 1942, just after leaving the desert. The nearest plane is being 'run up' with two airmen holding down the tail. *below*: The author's Hurricane being pushed out of the secret camouflaged hanger in Tobruk, November 1941.

one evening when a round fell very close. Everyone heard the scream and dropped to the ground, scrambling for places under the wooden tables. Apparently I continued sitting and eating. When the noise died down I said, with heavy sarcasm, "What are you stupid bastards doing under the tables?" I don't recall the incident, but it's a good story and is typical of my attitude. Why should a man destined to die in the air throw himself under a table?

When 451 Squadron was pulled out of the Western Desert in 1943, my C.O. sent for me. 'Wizard' Williams was a wily Welshman with a silken voice like Anthony Hopkins and possessed of great political ability. The army we supplied with aerial intelligence had no respect for the courage or integrity of airmen and they made reconnaissance requests which would have killed us all within a week. Wizard fought them off. I was grateful to him, and he to me—because he flew little and I flew much. The Australian pilots of this not completely Australian squadron had outspoken doubts about the military usefulness of Brits. Molly Malone and Pat Byers, the senior RAF pilots were shot down in the first few weeks. Micky Carmichael was hit in the head by a Messerschmitt cannon shell and was grounded for the remainder of the campaign. I alone was left to represent the regular RAF. I knew I had to out-fly the Aussies or the whole command structure would fall to bits. That, in a nutshell, is the theme of *Messerschmitt Roulette*.

"Geoffrey," Wizard said, smiling in his avuncular fashion, "You want to go back to India and get married."

It was a scene from a film that will never be made. Wizard with his Australian fur felt hat on the back of his head, pipe in mouth, leaning back in his chair to touch the canvas of his small office tent. Me, standing hatless and dirty, clothed in a ragged khaki uniform which was innocent of rank badges. He had arranged for me to fly a delivery Hurricane from Kilo 26 in Egypt to Karachi. This was my reward, and the end of our curious relationship. We both knew that our mission was accomplished. He had fought off the army and I had fought off the Australians. I never saw him again. But we are indivisible somewhere in history, locked in a time warp of the pressures of war.

A week later I was flying in a gaggle of Hurricanes to India, led by a Bristol Blenheim as mother goose. With no navigation to worry about, it was a joy to observe the desert regions of the Middle East, the majestic progress of the Tigris and Euphrates, and the ruins of Babylon. At Karachi, a northbound train took me overnight to Lahore. It was 4th March 1942.

I took a taxi to Major Lettington's ample residence in the cantonment, but Joan was at the military hospital. She had changed her job and was now on the nursing staff. I found her in a ward of sick soldiers, looking delicious in a white uniform, white stockings and white shoes. When she saw me she tore off her nurses cap and gave herself to me in the grand manner. The sick soldiers cheered.

"We can get married in a couple of day's time," she said, pushing me away from her. "You'll have to be a good boy till then."

No. 5 Squadron was no longer based at the Lahore airfield. Batts and Michael and Ericses Cawdreys and Willy Wilson and Johnny Haile were all in Assam, awaiting the Japanese assault. George Topliss, however, had by good fortune transferred to Lahore as senior equipment officer. He stood by me at the altar of the cantonment Catholic chapel on 7th March. Joan kept us waiting a long time. George and the bearded Father Roger made some jokes about Joan's harum-scarum temperament, while I wondered whether she was playing out some ancient game of feminine reluctance—though reluctance was not Joan's trump card. At last she rushed into the chapel, pursued by her father, his military hat in hand.

"The dress I ordered wouldn't fit," she gasped. "This is my sister Violet's, and it only fits where it touches!" Violet had been married a few months previously, in less hurried circumstances, to Alan Haig, an officer in the Indian Army.

Joan looked brilliant and fleshly in her sister's dress. It was too short for her and her bust could not complete with Violet's, but she was at the top of her form. Her smile was complete in its slightly exaggerated perfection.

The chapel was crowded with members of the Anglo-Indian community who had been praying for my survival for a year. Joan's mother had invited everyone to the reception. The women had adorned their dark skins with powder and rouge designed for lighter complexions, and the effect was to make their faces an unnatural purple colour. They embraced me in a cloud of cheap perfume. "Our prayers have brought you back," one said. I should have felt warm and grateful, but coping with sudden death on a daily basis is atrociously hardening to the spirit. I thanked them without conviction and regret those moment's now; but at the time my survival did not seem the right subject for prayer. Somebody had to be killed, why not me? Why Molly Malone and Pat Byers? Why Ken Whalley and Hugh Walford? Why Ian Porter and Miller Readett? Why those two South African stalwarts, Smith and Thomas? I have listed the known dead of No. 451 Squadron in reverence, but in 1942 I counted myself among them. I did not allow myself to hope that I would survive the war. In Joan's presence, however, I kept such convictions to myself. Our brief honeymoon was spent in considerable pomp and circumstance. Pat Biggie's brother Leslie was principal of the Indian Police College at Moradabad in United Provinces (now Uttar Pradesh) and he invited us to share the privileges of the yet unfaded British Raj. We were provided with a team of Ghurka servants to do our slightest bidding, and we attended some of the elaborate social events that seemed to occur on a daily basis in this environment. It seems ungrateful to say it, but it wouldn't have mattered where we had our honeymoon. To be together was enough. Time passed with the glassy efficiency of a movie. When we returned to Lahore Joan would not leave me; so we travelled together by train to Karachi and said our farewells there. The next day I boarded a 31 Squadron Dakota for the middle East.

Our wedding day, 7th March 1942, with Father Roger.

*   *   *

On my return to the Middle East I had been transferred to Rayak in Syria (No. 74 Operational Training Unit) which had been set up to teach reconnaissance techniques. I had been promoted to squadron leader and was second in command. Rayak had been a French military airfield and was now a RAF station. It was in the Bekaa Valley a few miles from Zahle, a pretty town on a hill half-way between Beirut and Damascus. Students began to arrive and I found myself teaching low level tactics, line overlap photography and artillery spotting. One of the students was John.W. Keller, an American in the RAF. He read *Messerschmitt Roulette* in 1994 and wrote to me to say that I had checked him out on a Harvard at Rayak before sending him on his first solo on a Hurricane. He remembers me as a rather glamorous figure, a beribboned survivor of past battles in the air. John had been at Harvard when the war broke out and was one of three in his class who volunteered to help Britain in her lonely struggle. He was taught to fly in Canada and arrived in the Middle East when Rommel was still rampaging and the military situation was desperate. After Rayak he was assigned to No. 680 Squadron, flying photographic Spitfires which penetrated enemy territory at high altitude. But before he had a chance to begin his operational career fate intervened and he found himself in—of all unlikely places—the Roosevelt white House. The story is best told in his own words.

> In July of 1942, 1 was being flown from Cairo to Beirut in a Lockheed transport to my final training school, the O.T.U. at Rayak, Syria, when I fell into conversation with a U.S. Army major. This gentleman— his name may have been Macaulay—drew me out in conversation and he appeared to enjoy getting to know this American in a foreign air force. The result of this chance meeting occurred a few months later in March 1943. He was based at headquarters in Cairo, and, when some documents were to be flown to Washington, he remembered my name and Squadron. He contacted me at Kilo Tamana, eight kilos outside Cairo, and asked if

Christmas Day 1943, at Tocra, Libya. The pilots were members of 'B' Flight 680 Squadron, Royal Air Force. All are in the Royal Air Force if not otherwise stated. *Rear row (l. to r.)*: Flying Officer Boyer (Administration), Flying Officer Gus Searle, Flying Officer John Keller (USA), Melvyn Howe (Photo Interpreter), Flying Officer Richie (Royal Canadian Air Force), Flying Officer Fox (Photo Interpreter, Middle East Intelligence Unit), unidentified, Flying Officer Chidgey (Photo Interpreter). *Front row (l. to r.)*: Flying Officer Pearson, Flying Officer Peter Mcgregor Walker (Royal New Zealand Air Force), Flying Officer Joe Owen (Royal Canadian Air Force), Flying Officer Lyn Mellor (Royal Australian Air Force, Flying Officer Ernie Ellison (DFC, MM).

I could be spared to act as King's courier to bring information to the RAF Mission in Washington. Being a slow learner in the art of photographing the pyramids from 28,000 feet, I was granted a leave of absence, too eagerly I felt. The documents needed a bit of study pertaining to the performance of the engines of the P-40 or Tomahawk in the Western Desert.

I was overjoyed at the prospect of seeing my wife once again, as I had embarked on a troopship out of Halifax three days after Pearl Harbor two weeks after our marriage. The mails were very slow so that I did not learn that I was to be a father until April of 1942, and Jeremy arrived in August 1942.

1 was issued a revolver and a document which stated that as a King's courier, I was allowed to "pass without let or hindrance" wherever I might be. I always liked that expression. With the help of the USAAF Air Transport Command, I was carried for the next week to Khartoum, Maiduguri, Chad in French Equatorial Africa, Accra, British West Africa, Ascension Island in the mid-Atlantic, Belem Brazil, Georgetown, British Guiana, San Juan, Puerto Rico and finally, Washington, D.C.

My wife and I were the two happiest people on any continent, and there was no doubt about that in either of our hearts. But then came the shocker! We were invited to dine and spend the night at the White House with the President and Mrs. Roosevelt on 3/14/43. My wife, Pat, and I had grown up with Mrs. Roosevelt's niece who had been a bridesmaid at our wedding. When the niece heard that I was coming to Washington, she had written to Aunt Eleanor pointing out how difficult it was to find a hotel room in wartime and asking her if she might be able to put us up. She had agreed, even though it was a Sunday night, the night of the official state dinner.

The cab driver looked in the back seat a second time when we said "To the White House please, without let or hindrance." We were ushered across the great seal in the hall and taken to our room on second floor—

upper left corner as you face the front facade. The bed had a plaque at the foot stating that this was the bed occupied by King George VI on the occasion of his visit in 1938. And in a small adjoining room, there was a bassinet set up for my seven months old son still in Boston. I was to have my first introduction to him the following day—an emotional summit and instant fatherhood!

A valet knocked at our door to ask if we wished our clothes to be smartened up a bit; after one week on the air transport command's route, it was obvious that there was a great need. We surrendered all, including shoes. Everything was returned within an hour, cleaned and pressed, and even the soles of my shoes with large holes had been polished. We were told that someone would come for us at 6:30 to take us to dinner, so we were prepared and looking at our best, or at least our best possible at the right hour.

But then, no one came. At about 7 p.m. we wandered out into the hall, deserted except for 'Falla,' FDR's dog. Finally, we were found and ushered down to where the president was supplying the guests with cocktails. I clutched my Manhattan with both hands to keep the meniscus level, but the trembling was hard to manage. As for the guests surrounding us, almost all had had their face on the cover of *Time*. I was in the uniform of a Pilot Officer in the RAF, the lowest commissioned rank, with my wings my only "decoration."

The rank and decorations of the guests were appalling. Admiral King, Admiral Leahy, Field Marshall Sir John Dill (Head of the combined chiefs of staff), Ambassador Winant, Anthony Eden—the faces and the ribbons went on and on. We were seated at opposite ends of the enormous table well below the salt, and I sat between General George Marshall and Harry Hopkins. At the short axis sat the President and Mrs. Roosevelt, Even then in the spring of 1943, the president was looking very wan and tired. We were served roast beef and Yorkshire pudding with ice cream for dessert, a far cry indeed from our mess at 680 Squadron in Cairo.

Harry Hopkins was expert at keeping the conversation rolling with this young man who felt very much out of his depth. We talked of the morale of the Middle East and the problems of deciding how much shipping should be devoted to beer and how much to munitions. I think that General Marshall found the Colonel on his left more interesting as he had been commanding the film crew that filmed *Desert Victory,* the advance westward from El Alamein and the beginning of the end for Erwin Rommel.

After dinner we adjourned to the theatre in the basement for the showing of the film, beginning with the sappers clearing the minefields with the bagpipes skirling in the night, And it was then that I made my only *faux pas*. I had been chatting with a dignified gentleman for a few minutes when he asked me my name, and then I reflexly asked him his. He was Sumner Wells, undersecretary of state. My wife, Pat, did better after John Winant of New Hampshire found out that he was a good friend of her grandmother's up in Center Sandwich, New Hampshire.

We breakfasted the next morning around a card table with Mrs. Roosevelt on the second floor, and returned to reality again. The RAF Commission informed me that the documents which I had studied and given them were quite self-explanatory, and why didn't I just take a nice long leave in New England? Again the world did not seem real, especially with the overwhelming sensation of meeting my firstborn son a few days later in Brookline.

After a leisurely leave of several weeks we received an invitation to another Sunday night dinner from Mrs. Roosevelt, and we figured that we must have used the right fork. We learned that Winston Churchill would be present, but my leave was to expire three days before the dinner! I have always regretted being the good soldier, foregoing the dinner with my personal hero and reporting for duty as ordered. It would have been so very pleasant to tell my eight grandchildren, gathered about my knees, about the night I asked the prime minister to forgive my sin of being AWOL in the White House.

Keller describes his tour of operations with No. 680 Squadron in modest terms:

> I was delighted to be flying the world's best aircraft, the Spitfire, behind the best engine, the Rolls Royce Merlin, and in the world's best air force. We flew unarmed, unpressurized, and, for the most part unafraid! At 28,000 feet. I flew 81 operations over Greece, Crete and the Dodecanese Islands, keeping an eye on German build up of supplies and troops, and no doubt providing targets for the bomber boys. On completion of 300 hours over enemy territory my nice C.O., Roger Whelan, DSO, DFC, recommended me for a DFC and a trip home, both of which were honored. Incidentally, I might not have been the first Keller to fight beside the noble British. My ancestors may have been Hessians who fought alongside the redcoats and then had to stay here for lack of funds to get back to Germany.

The Kellers were a military family. His father, an Annapolis graduate, was one of the commissioning officers of the United State's first aircraft carrier, the *USS Langley*, in 1920. His only brother was a regular officer in the navy and a lieutenant commander when he was shot down and killed.

> My older brother was demolished over Kyushu Island while dive bombing. He was a splendid athlete in college—all New England hockey and lacrosse— and had the reputation of being an excellent pilot, with 100 night landings on carriers. On his final sortie he was flying a Vought-Corsair off the *USS Wasp* as it stood 80 miles from the mainland of Japan in March, 1945.

SUPPER AT THE WHITE HOUSE*
Sunday evening, March 14, 1943
at 7:30 o'clock.

The President and Mrs. Roosevelt
T.R.H. The Crown Prince Olav
      and The Crown Princess Martha
The Right Honorable Anthony Eden, M.C., M.P.
H.E. The British Ambassador and Lady Halifax
The Secretary of State and Mrs. Hull
Hon. Sumner Welles (Acting Secretary of State)
Field Marshal Sir John and Lady Dill
Colonel J. J. Llewellin
Admiral Sir Percy and Lady Noble
Admiral William D. Leahy
General and Mrs. George C. Marshall
Admiral and Mrs. Ernest J. King
Ambassador John G. Winant
Colonel David McDonald
Hon. and Mrs. Harry L. Hopkins
Lieutenant and Mrs. J. W. Keller

Regrets:
    The Secy of State & Mrs. Hull
    Adm. Sir Percy and Lady Noble

* Reproduced from holdings at the Franklin D. Roosevelt Library.

John Keller in the
cockpit of his Spitfire.

Lt. Com. Russell Keller
standing in front of a
Douglas dive bomber.

Since the film, *Saving Private Ryan*, and Tom Brokaw's book, *The Greatest Generation*,[2] there has been renewed interest in the amazing heroism of the young Americans who fought in World War II. In this regard the Keller brothers could stand as a model—beyond praise or reward.

After the war John Keller became a physician and is now retired and lives at Nahant, Massachusetts. I have persuaded him to join the Royal Air Force Club, Piccadilly, where he finds himself much at home among the squadron crests and the trophies of two world wars.

---

[2] Tom Brokaw, *The Greatest Generation*. New York, Random House, 1998.

above (l. to r.): The Australian adjutant Bill Langslow, Squadron Leader R. D. 'Wizard' Williams, and 'Doc' Reid, the Australian medical officer.
below: Warming themselves in front of the bivouac tents are *(l. to r.)* an Australian stores officer; unidentified; Lt. 'Tommy' Thomas, SAAF; F/O Paddy Hutley, RAAF; and F/O Kevin Springbett, RAAF.

15

EGYPT

In late August I let it be known that I needed to go to Cairo because my brother Peter, a tank driver with the Royal Gloucestershire Hussars, was in the area re-equipping with new tanks after being trashed by Rommel's Panzers. My opportunity came when Major O'Sullivan, one of the army liaison officers on the staff at Rayak, had to attend a conference at G.H.Q. and I volunteered to fly him there. He was the brother of Maureen O'Sullivan whose fame stood high at the time. She had been the mate of Tarzan of the Apes in a film with Johnny Weismuller and she looked delectable in the remnants of a skirt. O'Sullivan was a short, good-looking man with dark wavy hair and a marked resemblance to his sister.

We took off early on 12th September, intending to spend the night at Shepheards Hotel and return the next day. The weather was poor over the Bekaa Valley, obscuring the tops of the hills. I could have kept low and sneaked through the passes into Palestine and thence to the coastal plain to Egypt. It would have been the prudent thing to do. I had not been in a cloud since Hullavington and my last instrument flying practice had been on the Link Trainer at Ambala in September 1939. Some hubris, some tragic flaw, some misbegotten imp of overconfidence persuaded me that this was the day to enter a cloud. When the cloud base was low. When the mountains were heaped unpredictably in my path. The basic skill to take off and land an aircraft can survive a long period of not flying. But flying by instruments alone, without the blessed orientation of a horizon, is another thing entirely. It requires constant practice. Even a month without it can land a pilot in trouble. I was grossly unready to tackle the inside of heavy cumulus clouds, lit occasionally by the weird deceiving patches of sunshine that hung over Lebanon that day.

"I'm going to climb over it," I shouted to O'Sullivan, as I shot through the wispy rags that drifted below the dark mattress of cloud, 800 feet above the valley floor.

The air was steady at first and climbing seemed easy. I stared at my instrument panel and let my eyes wander from the airspeed indicator to the altimeter to the turn-and-bank indicator, as I'd been taught. Ninety miles an hour. Throttle three-quarters open. In ten minutes, I thought, I'll be out on top.

The altimeter was registering a steady climb. 5000 feet. 6000 feet. 6500 feet. The highest mountain in the area was almost 7000 feet. I'd soon be safely above it. There was no artificial horizon fitted to this model of Harvard. Turn was shown by a bubble in a horizontal tube, like a thermometer. I was used to the Reid and Sigrist instrument, operated by gyros. The damned bubble put me off. On a fine day, with a sharp horizon ringing the visible world, I'd glanced at it without malice. Now it seemed an enigma. I couldn't 'see' the attitude of my aircraft. I began to doubt.

Suddenly the scene brightened. The murk changed to white haze. A flash of clear sunlight revealed a wall of towering cumulus, strangely angled.

Into the murk again

The impression I'd received from the momentary illumination was that my left wing was horribly down and that my nose was canted almost vertical. I made an instinctive correction, pushing the stick forward and levelling the wing. But as soon as I concentrated on my instrument again I knew it had been an illusion, for my turn indicator was full right and the speed had built up to 200 mph. The controls were already feeling stiff. I was in a dive, dammit!

Opposite rudder and aileron. Pull the stick back. Uneven air and the occasional severe bump made my task more difficult. I couldn't seem to be able to keep the bubble in the centre of its little tube. It flopped from side to side. I knew I was over correcting, but I couldn't stop doing it. Panic had set in.

I could feel myself being crushed against one side of the cockpit, as if the aircraft were careering sideways. A moment's break in the cloud revealed a frightening vision of my skewed Harvard glissading down a powdery slope. Then blankness, and the seemingly unending struggle to get on an even keel.

I was conscious of a growing hush, as if I'd gone deaf or the engine had failed. I checked my throttle setting and engine revs. Nothing amiss there. What about the airspeed? Christ! Fifty-five miles an hour! I was about to stall!

I jammed the stick forward against the instrument panel. It was too late to prevent a stall. I felt the kite flip on to its back, felt the weightlessness, then the heavy engine dropping the nose. I was in a vertical dive and out of control over high mountains.

"Is everything all right?" O'Sullivan asked politely.

I didn't answer him. I was about to smash both of us to smithereens.

A curious calm overtakes the mind when things are really hopeless. I had made a gross error of judgement and was going to pay for it with my life. Ah, well! Let us see if anything can be salvaged from the situation. If not it would be a quick death.

My altimeter was winding down briskly. I looked at the figures but could not interpret them. I looked at the wretched bubble and by what I felt were infinitely minor adjustments of my controls I managed to place it centrally in its tube. The scream of high speed was scary. Get that airspeed down. Back, back gently with the stick. Don't overdo it and end up pointing to the sky again. Let's hope the limestone slabs I'd seen on sunny days won't intervene and bring all the fun to an end.

I noticed a growing light. Then flashes of pure sunlight, blue edges of cloud. Then a glimpse of blessed earth. Directly below me was a cluster of red-tiled houses caught in a shaft of sunlight. I dived directly for that opening, keeping my eyes on the rooftops, turning this way and that to avoid the huge banks of cloud that threatened to close in on me. Steeper and steeper to keep that glimpse of green earth and red rooftop in view. The noise of speed, even with my engine throttled back, was frightening, but I knew I must thread my way towards the patch of sunlight that was striking the real solid earth, even if I smashed into it. Which I nearly did. I had to pull out of the dive suddenly to miss the stone walls of a slanted field above a Maronite village whose domed church blocked my path. I had to raise a wing to avoid it as I sped over the huddled houses and the narrow streets.

A second later I found myself in a big landscape. There was a broad and fertile valley before me and a grey mattress of cloud above me. I was safe. But there was a hush in my soul at the blasphemy of nearly killing a valuable front line pilot (me), not to speak of the innocent Major O'Sullivan, who was to be Mia Farrow's uncle![1]

---

[1] Strangely enough, I met Mia Farrow in the early Sixties, but failed to tell her the story of how I nearly killed her uncle. At the time I was commuting across the Atlantic for conferences in the Pentagon, and my American friends always arranged for me to fly 'space available' to Los Angeles on the small Presidential jets that ferried less important government officials around the country. Hugh French and his son Robin were riding high as agents for Richard Burton, Elizabeth Taylor, James Mason and other important actors. I would be met by one of their identical Bentleys and whisked off to Hugh's Malibu Beach house (bought on his death by Barbara Streisand) or to Robin's swimming-pooled eerie on the hills overlooking the city. Hugh introduced me to Richard and Elizabeth on the set of *Who's Afraid of Virginia Woolf?* and Robin took me to a beach party where I failed to tell my story to Mia because I was sitting, rather stunned, between Jane Fonda and June Havoc, the glamorous sister of Gypsy Rose Lee!

As we booked our rooms in the lofty marble foyer of Shepheards Hotel, filled with scampering porters in wide cut pantaloons and red tarbooshes, I found the courage to raise an anxious question.

"Did you enjoy the flight?" I asked timidly.

"Oh, yes," O'Sullivan replied. "I loved it when we were low down over those Lebanese villages."

He had not realized how close he had been to sudden death; bits and pieces of his mortal remains combined with aeroplane parts scattered over a barren mountain. A hurried military funeral in Haifa. Maureen's telegraphed flowers placed on his half empty coffin.

Peter was at the Gloucestershire Hussars' base depot at Abbasiyah near Cairo. We spent an afternoon and evening together. I have a picture of us, taken by a street photographer with Pete looking very professional in his black beret.

General Montgomery was shaking things up in the Middle East. One of the changes he made was that Peter's unit had to parade in shirts and shorts and run several miles each day. Everyone resented the order but Monty had an agenda that went beyond physical fitness. He was insisting that his commanders should be vigorous and that the incompetent ones should not be protected by hierarchical advantages.

The story was going round, Peter said, that Monty had turned up early one morning at the headquarters of a tank regiment. He had come to observe the run, he said. The officers and their men were all in their running togs, just about to commence.

"Where's the colonel?" asked the general.

"He's got a sprained ankle," the adjutant explained.

"Sprained ankles are no good to me," Monty said. "I'll send his replacement tomorrow."

By such no-nonsense tactics and by addressing large numbers of troops, he changed the somewhat defeatist tone of the

Two brothers, Peter *(l.)* and Geoff,
taken by a Cairo street photographer, 1942.

army to one of confidence. He was as unlikely a leader of men as the sickly Julius Caesar, having a speech impediment that turned all his r's into w's in the most comical way.

"We're going to hit Wommel for six," he would say, using a cricketing term. And mysteriously his soldiers believed him.

Much has been written since the war about the enormous reinforcements of armour that he demanded and received, compared to the slim resources of previous commanders, such as Wavell and Cunningham. He has also been criticized for being too conservative and too apprehensive of casualties, delaying his moves until he felt he had overwhelming superiority. But he had been a line infantry officer in the war of 1914-1918 and had seen a generation wiped out in the trenches. No British soldier that I know complained about Monty's sensitivity to the lives of his men.

There was something preposterous about him. He wore brown jerseys and corduroy trousers and his floppy tank beret was heavy with regimental insignia. He quacked away in the high penetrating tone of a science teacher at a private school. Yet he forced his army, which had experienced almost nothing but defeat since the beginning of the war, to believe it could win. Peter was just nineteen when he joined the army, and he had the longest front line war of all the Morley-Mowers. He arrived in Egypt with the Gloucestershire Hussars in October 1941, and a month later was knocked out of his Crusader tank by gunners of the Italian Ariete Division at Bir El Gubi.

"The Crusader tank," Peter writes, "was a medium tank with reasonable armour and a two-pounder gun as useful as a pea shooter. Rommel's Mark III and IV tanks equipped with the 88 millimetre gun could pick us off long before we got in range. It was a hopelessly unequal contest." In November 1941, the Gloucesters having lost all their tanks, were re-equipped with American Lend-Lease tanks. Peter describes them as follows: "They were 1927 type Stuarts, usually known as Honeys. Paper thin armour. A useless 37mm gun. No internal intercom.

Peter in the uniform of the Gloucestershire Hussars, Cairo 1942.

A converted radial aero engine. They burned beautifully!" In December 1941, the Gloucesters chased the retreating Germans and Italians as far as Agedabia, south of Benghazi, but Rommel counter attacked on 27th December. After suffering crippling losses of tanks the Gloucesters were pulled back to the Delta for re-equipment.

In June 1942, Peter, by this time a corporal tank commander, was part of a 'Jock Column'—a formation invented by the famous Brigadier General 'Jock' Campbell—comprising one platoon of motorized infantry, one troop of 25-pounder guns, and one troop of tanks. For a month they harrassed enemy supply lines and communications south of Tobruk. In August of the same year he drove a tank as part of a composite force which included the Scots Greys, opposing Rommel's so-called 'reconnaissance in force.' By this time the Gloucestershire Hussars had so many casualties that the regiment was disbanded! Peter was sent to the 8th King's Royal Irish Hussars, a regular unit with armoured cars stationed in Cyprus. It sounded like a holiday after the intense fighting in the Western Desert, but Peter took such a dislike to the regiment that he applied for a commission in order to avoid serving in it. He attended O.C.T.U. (Officer Cadet Training Unit) at Acre in Palestine and became a qualified machine gun officer.

In 1944, the focus of the war had moved to Italy and he joined the 2nd Bedfordshire and Hertfordshire regiment with the 4th British infantry Division. For the latter part of 1944 he fought on foot with a machine gun unit along the line of Via Emelia, Cesina, Bertinora and Salbagnone, called the Gothic Line. He ended up at Faenza in northern Italy. But his war was not yet over.

In December 1944, E.L.A.S. (the Greek People's National Party of Liberation), a Communist front supported by the Soviet Union, attempted a takeover of the Greek nation. Peter's unit was shipped to the Piraeus to clear Athens of E.L.A.S. troops

Joan and Geoffrey in Jerusalem, January 1943.

street by street. These were the most stressful months of his war. The opposition was not in uniform and innocent civilians could be caught in the crossfire. He remembers kicking open doors, never knowing whether he would face a hail of bullets or some cowering non-combatant. They pursued the Communists through Thebes, Lamia and Larissa until, in May 1945, he set up, with his friend Graham Martin a Brigade Battle School on the lower slopes of Mount Olympus. They lived in the presbytery of the local Orthodox priest.

His career is typical in another way. In spite of his long exposure to shot and shell he received no awards. A more sensitive military might have given him a decoration for survival!

Joan had joined me in the Middle East in November 1942, and we lived together in Jerusalem, waiting to return to England.

My brother Ken was also in Palestine. He had arrived early in 1941 as a corporal in the Intelligence Corps. At G.H.Q in Cairo he was interviewed by the head of the Greek section, Captain Lefoglu, a squat, cheerful devious homosexual who had spent his entire adult life as a British spy in the Balkans. For decades his 'cover' had been as a journalist in Belgrade. Born in Turkey of Greek parents, he could now openly proclaim himself a British citizen and, at the age of sixty-four, pensionable. Just before the war he had bought himself a cottage for his retirement in Devon. He took an immediate liking to Ken and quickly devised an interesting assignment for him. He was to be Lefoglu's informant in the Greek community of Cairo where German agents abounded. His new identity was to be a fanatical Irish nationalist who had been trapped in Egypt by the war. His role was to express loudly his hatred of Britain so that Axis spies would be drawn to him like iron filings to a magnet.

It worked quite well. Lef arranged to have Ken arrested for vagrancy by the civilian police. Once in a local gaol he was able to make friends with anti-British Greeks who had been purposely

above: Brothers Ken and Geoff in Thebes, Egypt, October 1941.
below (l. to r.): Peter, Ken, and Geoff in Cairo, October 1942.
Ken is in his spy persona.

arrested at the same time. When he was released from prison he joined this community of Greek-speaking traitors. There was no intention of detaining these people indefinitely. "I want to know who they are," Lef said. "Then I want you to watch them. To see that they don't get out of hand."

Several times during the campaigns of 1941-42 I would get three days leave from my squadron, park my Hurricane at Heliopolis airport, and join Ken on the boulevards of Cairo. We would often dine out with Lefoglu because he loved to be seen with young men. It was good, he said, for his sexual reputation. We made a strange threesome. With his service hat cocked at a Ruritanian angle and his side pockets stuffed with pipes, tobacco and a fat notebook, Lefoglu made a preposterously unmilitary figure. Ken was six feet tall, dark, with a big expressive mouth. He looked clever and dangerous in his dirty, white double-breasted jacket and black drainpipe trousers. A hit man, perhaps, or a brothel keeper, a Levantine trader whose business was not doing well. I wore an unpressed uniform I'd been wearing for months, washed occasionally in the salt waters of the Mediterranean. It had no badges of rank (they were lost with most of my original kit in the first headlong retreat from Rommel's tanks) and I could only be identified as an officer by my dusty service hat. We sat at outdoor tables of Greek restaurants owned by German sympathisers, and I listened to this ex-spy and my brother the double agent discuss the intrigues, betrayals, murders and mayhem of wartime Cairo.

In November of 1941, when Rommel was threatening the security of our Egyptian base, Ken was ordered to kill six enemy agents in the event of German forces reaching Cairo. At first he was fascinated by the job and amused by Lefoglu and the exotic deadly sleaze of the spy world. But in early 1942 Ken heard that Lefoglu was to be assassinated and he warned him that he was in danger. Lefoglu laughed it off. "Why should they kill me?" he asked, in his spittle-filled Balkan accent. "They will only have to deal with my replacement." Nevertheless, in January 1942, he was

Geoffrey Morley-Mower, Jerusalem 1942.

seized one morning in his apartment by one of the pro-Axis parties, known as 'The King's Party.' They drove him sixty miles into
the emptiness of the Western Desert and left him there to die of
thirst. He was found some weeks later, lying on the sand in his
military uniform, his empty briefcase beside him. He had accepted
his fate and had made no attempt to move from the patch of sand
on which he'd been dumped by his enemies.

Ken contemplated going on a rampage to avenge him. He
had a pretty good idea who had done it from the sneering faces he
saw in the cafes where agents gathered. He was diverted, however, by an offer to land him on the mainland of Greece by submarine to carry out sabotage and to act as liaison with Greek parti-
sans. He went on an explosives course and was instructed in demo-
lition; but the submarine was sunk in the Mediterranean before it
could reach Alexandria. This was a major disappointment. By
March 1942, I had been awarded a DFC and Peter had been
knocked out of his fourth tank. Ken felt that, as the eldest in the
family, he had avoided the real war while his younger brothers
were slogging it out in the front line. Impulsively he applied for a
commission in the infantry.

In January of 1943 Ken had almost finished his training at
the O.C.T.U. in northern Palestine and we arranged to meet in
Haifa. I didn't exactly have a competitive relationship with my
brother. He was obviously my intellectual superior and I was happy
to follow his lead. But I was proud of Joan's beauty and vitality,
and I was eager to show her off. Ken's lover in Cairo, Marti, was
married to a British intelligence officer in Jerusalem. She was tall
and lovely and Swiss and very much in love with Ken. She was, in
fact, pregnant with his daughter. After the war was over she
divorced her husband and returned to Switzerland. My father had
the photograph she sent of Ken's child (looking so like him)
on the mantlepiece of his study. I had met Marti a number of
times and knew of Ken's emotional entanglement and mixed

feelings. Their troubled love story was in contrast to my own uncomplicated solution to the problem of sex and love.

To meet Ken for our weekend in Haifa we had to take an Arab bus. The bus station was just outside the walls of the Old City and the vehicle was almost full when we arrived. We found two seats behind and across the aisle from the driver, a big unshaven man wearing an Arab head-dress. There was a hostile murmur from the other passengers as we entered, which I took to be directed at my British uniform. I looked around at the grim faces and smiled reassuringly at Joan, who was clearly anxious at our reception. We were the only non-Arabs on the bus and there were no other women.

As we sat down the driver made a threatening gesture, as if to order us off, but he thought better of it. He started up the engine and raced it noisily before setting off down the crowded street, scattering pedestrians. As he did so he picked up a tyre iron from the floor and began beating on a metal box beside him. This is going to be panic time, I thought, squeezing Joan's hand. She looked frightened and I put my arm around her in support.

It was the wrong thing to do.

My gesture set the driver on a rampage. He let out a scream of rage. Turning back to glare at us, he made a violent speech in Arabic, banging on his tin box for emphasis at the end of each period.

I removed my arm from Joan's shoulder.

There was an elderly man in the other aisle wearing European dress and I turned to him for help.

"What is he saying?" I asked.

"Jewish whore," he replied, scowling at me and then looking away. This was at once taken up by the driver..

"Jewish whore," he repeated. "Yais, Jewish whore!"

He carried on in a mixture of Arabic and English for some minutes. He had damaged the tin box beyond repair and he threw it aside, beating even more violently on the solid metal floor of the cab. Other voices joined his. The racket was deafening. I could hear the reiterated words, "Jew, Yehuda." As we ran into the open country and began to descend from the heights of Jerusalem into the plain below, his performance grew more elaborate and much more dangerous. He was driving too fast for the narrow winding road, skidding inches from steep embankments and threatening to lose control of the vehicle and kill us all. With his right hand he tore up a newspaper and with a cigarette lighter set it on fire, shouting and banging and scattering the flaming fragments in the air, miming the destruction by fire of all Jews.

At this point alarm began to spread among the more responsible passengers and a delegation hurried from the rear of the bus, intent on quieting the man down and saving their lives with ours.

Gradually he calmed himself, shouted out less frequently, and eventually shut up. By the time we reached the plain his face had settled into a sombre mask of sulky embarrassment. He did not look back or say another word all the way to Haifa.

I am not sure whether I can completely interpret the incident. Clearly the whole busload of Arabs believed that Joan was my Jewish girlfriend. When I put my arm round her shoulder the gesture offended Islamic propriety and seemed to them a provocation, a flaunting of foreign obscenity in the holy city of Jerusalem. Hence the driver's righteous frenzy. We represented the two things they most hated; British rule and Jewish immigration. It is possible that the turning point came when one of the passengers, hearing us talk in English and perhaps spotting her wedding ring, began to suspect that we were a legitimate married couple.

The atmosphere was too hostile for any retractions or explanations on either side. I was seething with indignation and it prevented me from saying, "This is my wife you're raving at. She's not Jewish, she's English." The hell with them, I thought. And they weren't going to apologize for fear Joan turned out to be Jewish after all.

At the bus station in Haifa we alighted in dead silence, the driver averting his gaze and the passengers looking on impassively.

Ken looked quite different from the shady figure in the dirty white coat of his Cairo days. His battledress was new, his trousers pressed to a knife edge, his boots gleaming. He complained bitterly that the training was boring and unnecessary; nothing but running, jumping and climbing endlessly over obstacles. He was eager to get into a fighting unit and match the experience of his warstained younger brothers.

Haifa is a fine city on the slopes of a great hill and you walk up long flights of steps between the roads that circle round the top. We had dinner at a hotel with picture windows that overlooked the city and the sea. We drank a great deal of Carmel hock. I was with the two people I loved best and happiness has no story.

On the way back to our hotel in the pitch darkness of wartime blackout we stepped off, arm in arm, down a long flight of steps, unaware of its existence. We had considerable momentum and for a second or two we were flying through the blackness as if a trap door had opened up beneath us. Then we began striking steps and bouncing off them, arriving at the bottom upright, uninjured and still arm in arm. We at once proclaimed it a miracle and the protection of higher powers..

Ken said goodbye to us after lunch the next day. He looked freakishly smart and fit, with his red face and his blanco-ed canvas belt. He had gone from one masquerade to another, but his pose as a Cairo spy had been more in character. I did not know that I would never see him again.

16

RETURN TO ENGLAND

During the first six months of 1943 the Battle of the Atlantic went very badly. In March the Allies lost 97 ships in the first twenty days. Admiral Doenitz's U-Boats had taken to hunting in 'wolf packs' and they were able to predict a convoy's position and assemble large numbers of submarines for a kill. Joan and I were alerted for three sailing dates, only to have them cancelled because the ships had been sunk. Eventually we were embarked at Port Said in the first week of July 1943. Our ship was one of a convoy of merchantmen and troopships, and it was escorted by frigates of the Royal Navy. We stopped at Madagascar, spent a week in Durban and four days in Cape Town, where we climbed Table Mountain like tourists. The food was various and excellent, a wartime surprise after the austere menus of the Middle East, where potatoes and meat were luxuries. The ship's library held out. We shared a cabin with another married couple and Joan used her diplomatic arts to book regular times for making love. We didn't give a damn about submarines.

Sailing up the west coast of Africa, one night two ships of our convoy were sunk. The crew decided not to disturb our sleep.

At breakfast the next day we were told the sad news. When we took our constitutional round the deck, two of the familiar shapes were missing. The latter part of the voyage was a long haul through the mid-Atlantic wastes, changing course frequently, before descending upon Liverpool from the Arctic regions. The Battle of the Atlantic must have raged round us, for many ships were sunk that month; but the thrill of sea travel, the unaccustomed luxury, and the pleasures of young love provided a perfect curtain against the fear of drowning!

After clearing the grimy docks at Liverpool we took the first train to London. I had expected my countrymen to show some signs of strain, to encounter bad manners and weary looks; but a metamorphosis had occurred under the hammer of war. Being beseiged, bombed and threatened with national extinction suited the English people. A surprising happiness had spread its crystal tide across the nation. The bombing, which had flattened acres of important buildings in the city centres as well as the suburbs, had also been effective in reducing the nasty social barriers between classes. There was a new democratic spirit which was encouraged by the universal call to work. Under Winston Churchill's defiant leadership the nation was welded more completely than when it was facing the Spanish Armada or the threat of Napoleon.

My father was working in Birmingham and could not get away, so it was my mother who met us at the London station. I was standing up in the corridor and spotted her, looking anxiously at the windows as the carriages sped past. She had aged noticeably during my five-year absence and seemed much frailer. Subsequently I grew accustomed to her altered appearance and saw her as a healthy woman in her middle years. But that first impression, and my emotional response to it, remains.

In the England of 1943, everyone worked.

My mother was off to the factory the day after our arrival. It was a small firm in North Ealing on the Great West Road, called

Traper's Paper Tubes, and it manufactured long-range tanks for aircraft, cartridge cases and other paper products. Joan had to sign up for war work immediately. She asked to go to the same factory as my mother and they toddled off every morning, swinging their lunch baskets. I was still on leave and felt a bit out of it, waiting for my next call to arms.

One of the great blessings of that period was that my mother at once took to Joan. She was not a perfect housekeeper and for many years had employed two servants. Marjory, our maid of all work, had blossomed out to become the manageress of the Lyons tea shop in Ealing Broadway. She had come from a poor section of town and when she first came to us at the age of fifteen, my mother had immediately burned all her clothes and put her in our long bath to be thoroughly cleaned and baptized into a new life. She was now a young woman, well paid and married to a sergeant in the army. Marjory had long been the home disciplinarian. Wthout her (for servants had disappeared forever at the outbreak of war) my mother was at a loss. She would tidy up by stuffing things under the sofa or beneath seat cushions. She was terrified lest Joan would be revolted by the chaos in which she existed. But Joan was used to servants picking up after her, and she was not tidy by nature. Her method of undressing was always to discard her clothes directly on to the floor. So their styles were a perfect match. They became close friends and collaborators, united in their carelessness against the tidy world of women.

It wasn't long before Joan, with her characteristic energy, had become a star performer on her machine. Security was tight in the workplace, but she assumed she was making cartridge cases. One week she won an award for high productivity and decided to ask the foreman exactly what weapon of war she was producing.

"I know our work is secret, Mr Barton," she said, "but it would give me a lot of satisfaction to know how I'm contributing to the war effort."

"Your machine 'aint classified, Joan," he replied. "You're making the insides of toilet rolls!"

At the beginning of November 1943, I reported to Fighter Command Headquarters, Bentley Priory, with a speech prepared. I was rested from my Western Desert experience and certain that I would be offered the command of a recce squadron. In England the Hurricane had been replaced by a much swifter aircraft, the American P-51, which we called the Mustang. I dreamed of slashing across northern France, dodging flak and fighters, and blowing up the occasional train. To this day I hate the memory of Bentley Priory.

It was a large Victorian residence which had been chopped up into offices. The P Staff office was on the second floor at the top of a narrow servants' stairway, reminding me of the dismal aspect of my headmaster's study where punishment was meted out.

A cold young squadron leader with a DFC interviewed me.

"What do you want to do?" he said, giving me a weary smile.

I laid out my case. A long tour in North Africa working with the army surely gave me unique value. No recce pilot in Fighter Command had comparable experience because the British army had been bottled up in the UK since Dunkirk. I had a right to command one of those Mustang squadrons and show them how. Ideal candidate, in fact. Rested, ready and well informed.

He hardly seemed to be listening.

"You don't understand our position," he said, when I'd finished. "You are no doubt well qualified, but we have squadrons with six supernumerary squadron leaders attached to them. Those guys are all waiting for a job, and they have a better right than you because they're Fighter Command people. We couldn't possibly jump you to the top of the list. There'd be a riot."

"I'd like to see the wing commander," I said.

The wing commander was middle aged and bald and beady eyed. He gave me short shrift.

"I appreciate your feelings," he said, "but you're the right man in the wrong place. I suggest you go to Flying Training Command. They actually need people like you. When the balloon goes up, we may call on you."

I couldn't accept that. I insisted on being sent to an operational squadron. I could just taste those Mustangs. My luck would surely hold.

It didn't.

They posted me to No. 26 Squadron at RAF Church Fenton, in the flat country north of London where the Morleys and the Mowers once farmed land. I did not like the place and remember the sky as being perpetually overcast, curtained by my personal gloom. Disappointment has buried the details of my life there with such merciful efficiency that I can recall very little. There were other supernumerary squadron leaders and the training schedule did not include any of us. We had to beg for flights from the C.O., who often had good reasons for being unable to comply.

The P-51 was a superb aircraft. It zapped along with a solidity the Hurricane did not possess and the pilot got an all-round view from the bubble hood. I managed to do some air firing at a towed drogue. I flew an artillery shoot with some bored gunners at Larkhill. Mostly, I just hung around.

In four miserable months I managed to fly only seventeen hours on the Mustang and I grew to hate the smug faces of the regular pilots. They were training for the Second Front and nobody was in the least interested in my archaic desert war. I remember the exact moment I decided to go. A Canadian W.A.A.F. officer was departing the station, having married someone in a bomber squadron, and the mess gave her a farewell party. I stood on the outskirts of this gathering, feeling lonely without Joan and thinking how beautiful this girl managed to look in her blue uniform with the Canada flashes, her grey lisle stockings and sensible shoes. Lucky bomber boy, I thought. She's leaving. I must leave too.

The C.O. was relieved to know of my decision.

"I'm so glad," he said, grinning happily at me. "Didn't like to suggest it myself. Know you're disappointed. We're chockerblock with extra bods. We really couldn't cope with you."

A large impressive building filled with people on their best behavior is a terrifying place, even if one arrives in a taxi. In June 1944 1 was summoned to Buckingham Palace to receive the DFC I had been awarded for my work with 451 Squadron. Joan and my father went with me and watched the ceremony. It was quite a cosy affair, not more than thirty officers of all three services, and it didn't take long. The only person I recognized was Loppy Lerwill. I had last seen him running at the head of his Tochis in a khaki turban. We didn't have time to do more than greet one another in the large ornate anteroom, before ushers assembled us in due order and the King walked in.

We were in our best uniforms, but hatless, for it was an indoor ceremony. Family members were seated in rows of chairs behind us. George VI had a terrible stutter, but he spoke to each officer as he pinned on the decoration.

He saw my Indian Service Medal.

"Ah," he said, frowning slightly. "I see that you've b-b-been in India."

"Yes, sir."

"B-But your DFC is for the M-Middle East?"

"Yes, sir."

"W-W-Well done."

"Thank you, sir."

I wondered, looking at the reddish tinge of his skin, whether he been made up, like an actor for a stage appearance, but he moved on before I could be certain.

There were taxis to whisk us away from the gates of the palace. My father stood us a lunch at Simpsons.

*   *   *

My brother Ken was in Italy, a lieutenant in the London Irish Rifles. He wrote to me saying how appropriate it was for him to fight in an Anglo-Irish regiment. "I represent the historical ironies as well as anyone," he observed. "Some of our forefathers died for Dark Rosaleen and others cheerfully enslaved their children." In January 1944, his unit was part of the British First Division, under General Mark Clark's U.S. 6th Corps. On 22nd January they landed 30 miles south of Rome and fanned out to take Anzio and Nettuno, two little fishing villages used by the Romans for holidays by the sea. Hitler could not let the city of Rome fall without a struggle. He assembled the 14th Army to oppose the bridgehead. In a month of desperate fighting to sustain their foothold the Allies suffered 19,000 casualties. 2000 died, one of whom was my brother Ken.

When the fatal telegram was received, Joan came to Church Fenton to give me the news in person. We went for long walks in rainy weather while I digested the fact that I would never see him again. I couldn't get out of my mind a verse he had written during his last year at school. I hadn't liked it at the time because it sounded too close to an epitaph.

> Better to fall like a falling star
> Than rise like the pallid moon,
> Bright with the sun's reflected light,
> But never a light of its own.

I wasn't sorry for him in the conventional sense. He had been wiped out in an instant by a direct hit from a shell and not much of his body was recovered. There is a white cross with his name on it in the War Cemetery at Minturno[1] which is planted over nothing but

---

[1] Lieutenant John Kenneth Morley-Mower, 277673, 1st Bn. The London Irish Rifles, aged 28, is buried in Minturno War Cemetery, Plot V, Row F, Grave 5. Minturno is about 150 miles south of Rome.

above: Michael and Sheila Savage, 1944.   *below*: The author in the 1934 Austin Seven he bought in 1943. It outlasted the war and was sold in 1949 when he was given command of 224 Squadron at Gibraltar.

a sack of Italian earth. The grief was all for myself. I would now have to do without him; though that is a simplification. Fathers and mothers, and some elder brothers have a way of being eternally present, like guardian angels or the presence of God.

In 1944 the air attacks on London included standard night bombing and also 'Doodle Bugs.' Doodle Bugs were pilotless aeroplanes filled with high explosives that the Germans launched across the Channel to the city. They were jet propelled and their engines had a curious beat. You could recognize the sound miles away and everyone listened, waiting for the engine to cut out. When it did, there was a pause as it glided to the earth, making a terrific crump on impact. Strangely enough they weren't as frightening as a conventional bombing raid, even though their potential for destruction was greater. One could be sociable about them, speculating on the chances of them landing on Acton or Ruislip.

A bomb had demolished St Faith's Nursing Home where my twin sisters had been born, and the same bomb had cracked one of the outer walls of our family home. Temporary wooden supports had been erected to prevent collapse. My parents slept in a bedroom on the second floor and they did not usually get out of bed when a raid was in progress. However, when the weather was good and an attack was expected they would wander around talking to the air raid wardens. I once overheard a conversation between my mother and Mr Simpson, who owned the sweetshop on Pittshangar Lane. He was now the chief warden for our district. There was warning of a raid and the sirens were wailing.

"The Hobsons had to move out of number twelve, Mrs Mower," Mr Simpson was saying. "Very sad at their time of life."

"Well, they were both over seventy," my mother replied. "They'll be much safer in the country."

"This is going to be a big one, mark my words ... . When they start this early, we're for it!"

Neither of them seemed the least bit concerned. They might have been talking about the weather.

The pubs remained crowded. The trains ran. People walked about during air raids as if they were merely electrical storms. Joan was working in a war factory in London while I was learning to be a flying instructor at Upavon in Wiltshire and I'd drive to London when possible in my battered 1934 Austin Seven to renew my Fighter Command contacts. A pub in Shepherd Market in Mayfair was the unofficial headquarters of the fighter boys. I worked the bar, chasing my dimming hopes of a command, and getting pretty drunk in the process. Joan loved the exciting company of the Battle of Britain heroes, with the top buttons of their uniform jackets undone to show their superiority to other mortals. We met a wild-eyed girl there who had the misfortune to live near the fighter base at Biggin Hill. She had been engaged to marry six fighter boys and they had all failed to return from sorties.

One Saturday night we emerged at closing time to find London in flames. Walking to the Green Park tube station reminded me of the Tobruk scene. The underground system was packed with people taking refuge for the night. I had never seen it before. Families with their pillows and bedding were packed like sardines on the platforms. The trains were running in spite of the pandemonium at ground level. At Ealing Broadway station we made our exit into a classic German raid. Searchlights on Ealing Common cut the sky. Anti-aircraft guns cracked and whistled. Bombs were dropping from invisible bombers and fires were burning on all sides. We were not at all aghast. No sex for a month blotted out the raid from the forefront of our minds. It was half a mile to my father's house where a bed waited for us in what used to be the servants' quarters on the third floor. But half way up Mount Park Road was a site that had been bombed the previous year, a gap in the row of middle class dwellings. The foundations had grassed over and looked inviting in the sky's red glare. We turned aside into the ruins without a word, lay down and made love.

Joan was not the girl to care about a muddy skirt or stockings. We lay like Zeus and Hera on a golden cloud, while the nose caps of 3.7 inch anti-aircraft guns fell musically and murderously to earth and German bombs exploded dramatically a few streets away.

All my closest friends were in the thick of it. Pratap Lal was commanding Vultee Vengeance dive bombers in faraway Burma. George Topliss was flying Mosquitoes in No. 2 Group, attacking targets over Germany. Batts Barthold was commanding a wing of Spitfires somewhere north of London. The U.K. friends all commanded aeroplanes and could drop into each others' airfields to keep in contact. Michael Savage headed a daylight ground support squadron based on the North Downs, not far from the Channel coast. He wrote to me on 22nd July 1944:

> I think I may have told you that Sheila is coming as well, to live at Woodvale until we get hauled into the front line again. This is a peaceful and soul-healing spot, despite the endless stream of Hun projectiles that hurl themselves over the top of us. Otherwise it is all cows and buttercups and Sussex yokels, and the air is full of the soft swishing sound of the wind as it blows through the corn. Yesterday there was a soft swishing sound over the telephone, which was Batts ringing up from his station north of London. He has some adventurous scheme of coming down in an Auster and landing in the next field, so I hope I see him shortly. Sheila sends her love—I must stop and go out to watch a 'doodle.'

I flew in to see him on 3rd March 1945. Dunsfold was an idyllic spot of earth on the high treeless chalk downs, its beauty counterpointed by the odd shapes of Hawker Typhoons which sat dispersed in their bomb shelters. They looked to my eye like grownup Hurricanes, squatting on their haunches and appearing slightly overfed. I said as much to Michael as he drove me round the airfield.

"Beauty, my dear fellow," he replied, "is not the last word in this business. I see that your attitude towards flying is still aesthetic and unreformed. You need more lectures from Batts. Regard those two 20mm cannons projecting from each wing. The rocket rails slung below carry eight 3-inch weapons of destruction. This is the ultimate ground attack machine."

Afterwards we walked a mile down the narrow country road to the village with its single pub. It was crowded with uniformed men and women, but we managed to find corner seats and were soon lost in talk unconscious of the noise around us. Michael was pouring out poems and thought he might have enough of them for "a slim volume." We discussed old George Topliss' leap into the air battle and Batts' great eminence as a Spitfire leader. Michael had married Sheila Harvey in Dibrugarh, Assam, in 1942 and she was pregnant with 'Carolipher.'

"The baby kicked out during the fifth act of *Hamlet*, Michael said. "We think he's going to be a dramatic critic!"

I flew back to Lulsgate Bottom the next day in my beat-up Airspeed Oxford, envying Michael his poetry, his 'Carolipher' and his ugly but formidable aeroplanes. On 30th March I received a short sad letter from George Topliss. Michael had been killed on the 19th of that month while carrying out rocket attacks on targets in Northern France. I was scarcely surprised. The best and brightest, British and American were dying all around him on the Second Front. But I felt Michael's death almost as bitterly as Ken's.[2]

---

[2] As a grace note to a sad story it is good to know that Sheila married again and now lives in New Zealand with her husband. 'Carolipher' turned out to be Caroline, and she writes to me from Sydney, Australia, where she lives with her husband and a family of boys.

17

AFTER THE WAR

As soon as the war ended in September 1945, the peacetime bureaucratic machinery began to grind exceeding small and to threaten my career as a pilot. Within six months I was informed in a curt—and I thought insulting letter—that I was no longer a flyer because my eyesight had been discovered to be below standard. A formal message arrived written in the cold diction of British government fiats. "Sir, I am directed to inform you that your medical category does not permit you to remain in the General Duties Branch (*i.e.*, the flying branch) now that hostilities have ceased." Without consultation I had been assigned to the equipment branch, a role I most deeply feared. To me it meant deskwork, boredom and denial of the freedom of the skies while ironically wearing the blue uniform of the airman.

By this time I was working in the Directorate of Flying Training at Richmond Terrace, Whitehall. It was a lovely 18th century building which had been ineptly converted into offices and was opposite the India Office and Downing Street. The director was none other than Basil Embry, the heroic former commander of No. 2 Group. Ray Harries, a Battle of Britain fighter pilot, short and vibrant, shared my office. Nearby was a pal of Ray's, the top-scoring fighter ace Johnny Johnson. Basil Embry's personal assistant was another distinguished airman, Peter Wykeham. Alan Deere, the New Zealand ace, would pop in to talk and grumble about post-war austerity. We were all hanging around doing staff jobs while waiting to get flying commands. Every one in the department was famous except me; but we were all survivors and the mood was generous.

When the letter turned up in my 'In' tray and I read the first paragraph, I let out a bellow of disgust. "What the hell is this?" I shouted, drawing a friendly crowd from neighbouring offices. "So I can fly in the war but not in peacetime! What kind of logic is that?"

"Ungrateful bastards!" said Ray, whose cheerful aggressiveness could always be relied upon. "I'd fight it."

"How can I do that? Get a new set of peepers?"

"Appeal to the Monarch," said Ray. "He's well known to be soft on the flying boys."

The assembled princes of the skies growled their agreement.

"Appeal to the bloody Monarch," they chanted. "What have you got to lose?"

Ray should know, I thought. King George had been pinning gongs on his chest at yearly intervals throughout the war. He had two DSOs and three DFCs and must have been up at the palace at least five times. I started to write my first protest minutes after this informal gathering had dispersed.

The strength of my case, as Ray Harries had seen, was in the character of King George VI. He had been taught to fly as a young man and had been awarded his wings as a RAF pilot. During the war the general public most often saw him proudly wearing his RAF uniform. He had stayed in the capital city, braved the bombs like other Londoners, and it is not surprising that he identified strongly with the pilots who had saved the nation. He was soft on the RAF. Perhaps he'd be soft on me.

I could not appeal directly to the king, even though I held a commission signed by him. We were all members of 'His Majesty's Armed Forces,' though. Parliament was the supreme authority, but the fighting services traditionally belonged to the crown. I had the right to appeal, but only as a last resort.

The process was agonizingly slow. Like all bureaucratic procedures it moved in stages, punctuated by long pauses. I was medically examined and rejected as unfit. Then a letter arrived informing me that I was an equipment officer (untrained) and would shortly be removed from my job flying a desk in Whitehall. I refused to accept the decision of 'the board' and my appeal reached up to a higher rung on the ladder. Finally I was interviewed by a member of the Air Council. It took a whole year to reach this crisis point.

Air Marshal 'Black Mac' McDonald was the Air Member for Personnel, the apex of the administrative pyramid. Beyond Black Mac was the king. I was ushered into his office in Kingsway by a creepy personal assistant and the air marshal leapt to his feet, escorting me to a settee which stood beside an oak table some distance from his working desk. The table was polished to a glassy perfection. Neatly painted models of RAF aircraft were lined up from one end to the other—a Handley Page Hampden chasing a De Havilland Mosquito chasing an Avro Lancaster chasing a Supermarine Spitfire. He was a generation older than I and had spent the last five years directing the war from headquarters offices, not fighting it in the air. I had chosen to wear my uniform for this encounter, while he was smartly turned out in a dark blue pinstriped suit. I was conscious of having a slight edge.

"Well, young man," he said, smiling at me in a friendly manner. "I must congratulate you on your persistence. Candidly most people would not go as far as this. But here is the report of the latest medical board. They've shot you down again."

He handed me some papers I had seen many times before, always worded the same way. "Unfit for flying duties."

"So that's that. I'm really sorry. I'm sure you'll settle down happily in the equipment branch." He had dark wavy hair plastered back, very blue eyes and a blue chin where the morning razor had done a good job on his beard. He looked genuinely sorry, but I felt that his cheerfulness was put on to get me to accept his verdict. This was my moment. I had been rehearsing my utterance for weeks, and I trotted out my lines like a ham actor.

"I understand," I said, "that as an officer in His Majesty's Armed Forces I have a right to appeal to the king personally if I feel I have been unfairly treated in a serious matter. I now want to do that. I have proved my ability to fly under war conditions. I cannot see how I can now be rejected for the peacetime air force. If I am allowed to put my case before the king, I will abide by any decision he makes."

The air marshal had been sitting fairly close to me on the settee, leaning forward. I could smell what I thought was his shaving cream. Suddenly he threw himself backwards with a roar of laughter.

"By God," he shouted. "You have a bloody nerve. I've read your file and could hardly believe it. You've held us up to ransom. You're a naughty boy."

"Can I go back to flying, sir?" I asked.

"Oh, my God, yes," he said. "We would never trust you in front of King George. We know exactly what would happen. He'd ask you where you'd fought. He'd wring all sorts of confessions of heroism out of you. Then he'd call up the Air Council and cane our backsides for not respecting the generation that saved England."

So ended, in unlikely victory, my rather preposterous deception. In old age I am surprised at my younger self for having attempted it. But the closest I had got to complete failure was when Drip Williams had put me up for a rejection flight at Anstey.

The fates had favoured me then with a crowded circuit and three good landings. Flight Sergeant Boyd had caught me out fairly, but he had misinterpreted my blindness as stupidity. The outbreak of war protected me from dismissal by an annual medical examination. If I had known at the outset that my eyes were to be checked annually, I do not think I would have possessed the hardihood to push through my scheme. I was just young and ignorant.

After the interview I walked back across London from Kingsway to Whitehall, exalted at my escape from the equipment branch. Ray Harries spread the news during the afternoon and when work ended at 6 pm a posse of the most intrepid airmen in the Royal Air Force celebrated the occasion at a local pub where we often had lunch. It had a basement bar with a piano in it and Ray was in his best form, knowing the words to every song. I'll never forget that party or the generosity of those attending, all better men than I and worthy of their considerable fame.

Ray Harries didn't last long after the war was over. As commanding officer of a Vampire jet fighter squadron he flew back from a guest night at a neighbouring station in bad weather. He ran out of fuel over his closed down airfield, turned the kite on its back and dropped out. His parachute caught up in the Vampire's twin booms and Ray was dragged to earth with his plane.

Thanks, Ray, for a grand party.

Black Mac kept his promise to the naughty boy who had pulled the legs of the Air Council. Six months later I was piloting a Handley Page Halifax over the Bay of Biscay, on my way to take over command of No. 224 Squadron at Gibraltar. It was a much sought after posting. Enough flying to weary the most eager lover of flight and relief from the austerity of postwar Britain. It was the blue Mediterranean, where off duty hours could be spent at the yacht club, racing Sharpies and airborne lifeboats in the harbour or across the bay to Algeciras. In 1951, I converted

Geoffrey Morley-Mower while commander of
224 Squadron at Gibraltar in 1948.

all the squadron pilots from the old beatup Halifaxes we were flying to the new Avro Shackletons, with their counter-rotating props and sophisticated submarine tracking devices. There was some debate whether it was safe to do this from the Gibraltar airfield. The neck of land that joins it to Spain has only enough room for a connecting road and a customs post. The single runway had been built out into the bay, with water at both ends. Brake failures could be fatal. All circuits had to be flown laboriously round the huge limestone Rock, and nearly every landing was crosswind. Teaching pilots to fly a more complicated aircraft under such circumstances would be quite a circus. But I argued strongly for doing this, rather than taking the aircrew away from their families for six months to the chill of Ballykelly, Northern Ireland. In the event no accidents occurred and I was awarded the Air Force Cross for the good behaviour of my crews. King George VI died in February 1952, and it was his daughter, the very youthful Queen Elizabeth, who pinned the gong on my chest in Buckingham Palace that summer.

I apologize to the reader for touting this information. It sounds immodest. But I was grotesquely pleased by the award, and I chuckle to myself remembering it. It was, after all, the conclusion of my struggle. I may have been a fool to join the air force in the way I did, but perseverance paid off. I had, somehow, not very spectacularly justified myself as a pilot both in war and in peacetime. And since flying is such an ungraspably beautiful thing, superior to its technology—somewhere between a skill and an art and a pure exercise of the imagination—success in the air seems to take precedence over lesser honours, like receiving a degree or even getting a book published.

APPENDICES

Wedding of Squadron Leader Bertram Barthold and
Diane Sharp at St. Saviour's Church, London SW 3.
The author *(extreme r.)* was best man.

APPENDIX A
Bertram Barthold

Batts Barthold left No. 5 Squadron in 1942 and went on to command No. 146 Squadron in Assam, with Michael Savage as his flight commander. On his return to England in 1943 he was C.O. of two front-line squadrons in succession, Nos. 611 and 501. During the invasion of Europe in 1944 he commanded a mobile wing and ended up as part of the 2nd Tactical Air Force in Germany.

In 1948 he married Diana Sharp at St. Saviour's, London, and on that happy occasion I was Batts' best man. They had three daughters, Merryn, Rachel and Ann. He retired from the air force in 1967 as a group captain and lived beside the ocean at Constantine Bay in Cornwall, teaching at a preparatory school in Truro.

I last saw him when my wife Mary and I stayed with the Bartholds while we were on holiday in England in 1976. He was his old self, full of enthusiasm for his teaching, his garden, painting in oils which he'd just taken up, and the tales for children he was writing. He still treated me like a silly younger brother, and Mary loved them both instantaneously. He died of a heart attack in 1977. *Sunt lacrimae rerum.*

APPENDIX B
George Topliss

When George Topliss was best man at my wedding in 1942, I did not know that he had already made the first move towards becoming a pilot. In the summer of 1941 he had taken leave and obtained an 'A' License at the Karachi Flying Club. Although this certificate only permitted him to fly light civil aircraft, it must have convinced the people at the RAF Headquarters in Delhi that he was in dead earnest. In the fall of 1942 he was sent for initial flight training to Ambala. This was exactly the same weeding out process that I have described in Chapter 1. He had no difficulty with the course and was afterwards trained as a fighter pilot on Hawker Hurricanes at Risalpur, where he had once been senior equipment officer. By this time his rank had been reduced to pilot officer. In the winter of 1942-43 he returned to England by sea, when the German U-Boat campaign was at its height. A short stint flying Bristol Beaufighters in the night fighter role took him to No. 2 Group, headed by Air Vice Marshal Basil Embry, a legend in the RAF for courage and intrepidity. In 1940 Embry had been shot down over France and captured by the German army. He escaped and returned to his squadron, having slaughtered some of his captors. The Germans marked him as a war criminal, forcing him to fly pseudonymously as Wing Commander Smith!

No. 613 Squadron, to which George was assigned, was a night interdiction squadron equipped with the De Havilland Mosquito, a speedy lightweight machine constructed entirely of wood and powered by two Rolls Royce Merlin engines. While he was operating from Lasham in Wiltshire, I flew up with his current girfriend, a gorgeous WAAF officer who, to the disappointment of his friends, he did not marry. Most of George's sixty-six operational sorties were over Germany in the night interdiction role or straight bombing, but in September 1944, he took part in the famous daylight raid on Gestapo headquarters at Egleton in France, This was one of the raids led by Basil Embry as Wing Commander Smith. George was awarded the Distinguished Flying Cross in 1944.

After the war George opted not to return to the equipment branch, in spite of tempting offers of rank advantage. He flew Dakotas on the Berlin airlift in 1948, commanded RAF Dalcross in Scotland, flew Gloster Meteor and Javelin jet aircraft, and finally the Hawker Hunter, the most advanced of contemporary subsonic fighters.

He retired from the Royal Air Force in 1963 as a wing commander and became secretary of the College of Air Training, a flying school for airline pilots situated at Hamble on the Solent. He retired from this job in 1977. From 1969 to 1984 he carried out the duties of Magistrate and Justice of the Peace on the Southampton bench. He now lives with his wife, Eda, in the Dorset village of Portesham overlooking the English Channel.

APPENDIC C
Pratap Chandra Lal

After our animated discussion on the woman question at Karachi, Pratap Lal carried out his campaign to get married, war or no war. He asked his father to find him a suitable wife. His family belonged to the Brahmo Samaj, an idealistic society started by Raja Mohan Roy in 1826. It was a broad reformist movement which aimed at purifying Hinduism of social evils, like the burning of widows on the funeral pyres of their dead husbands. Along with the moral activism it included a literary dimension, with major figures such as Rabandra Nath Tagore. Clearly the lady would have to share the same faith. The candidate was Ela Ghosh (known as Hashi to her friends), and she answered all Pratap's requirements. She was nice looking, she possessed a degree in English literature, and she shared one language with him. Her native tongue was Bengali and his was Urdu. Their common language was English. After the introduction they liked one another and agreed to marry in late December 1941. This plan was frustrated by the Japanese attack on Pearl Harbor. All military leave was cancelled. Hashi writes:

> My mother had a nervous breakdown. The invitations had been printed and sent off. Well-wishing uncles advised me either to break off the engagement or wait till the end of the war. I thought that was not fair on me, and I protested. Three months later, in March 1942 my parents and I came to Delhi from Bengal and we were married.

Pratap joined No. 7 Squadron, Indian Air Force and soon was its commander. Re-equipped with Hawker Hurricanes, the

above: Pratap Lal *(center)* with Prime Minister Indira Ghandi, October 1969.   *below*: Pratap Lal at his desk as Commander-in-chief of the Indian Air Force, 1969.

squadron flew ground attack sorties against the Japanese until Rangoon was taken on 3rd May 1945. Pratap was awarded a mention in Despatches in 1944 and a Distinguished Flying Cross in 1945. He flew 210 operational hours against the enemy.

The remainder of his life was more dramatic than any of his wartime adventures, for his brilliant gifts raised him quickly in rank and set him against the politicians. He spent the rest of his days striving after virtue and truth, like the Red Crosse Knight in Spenser's "Faerie Queene." As a group captain he had to purchase some aircraft for the I.A.F. The deal had been arranged by the Indian High Commissioner, V.K. Krishna Menon, a friend of the Indian prime minister, Jawaharlal Nehru. Menon had been a longtime resident in England and had at one time been mayor of Paddington. The purchase proved to be a fiasco and Pratap, defying Menon's wrath, turned it down. Three of us dined together in London during this period, the third person being Kushwant Singh, the novelist. I remember Pratap described Menon scornfully as "that Paddington Street Communist!" His opposition to this powerful man had fateful consequences in his subsequent career.

In 1957 he was loaned by the air force to become general manager of Indian Air Lines, whose development into a major carrier was a government priority. Once again he clashed with Menon, who had become Defence Minister. Menon had been friend and political associate of British Labour Party politicians for most of his life, and he had sentimental motives for wishing to buy the British AVRO H.S.-748, which was in an early stage of development. Pratap knew that he needed immediate replacement for his ageing war surplus DC-3s, and he made a strong case for the Fokker-27, which was ready for delivery. Menon objected and Pratap took the matter to the Prime Minister. He won, but Menon vindictively sacked him, ending for several years both his civil and military careers. However, in 1963 the 'Young Turks' in the Indian parliament threw Menon out, and Pratap returned to the air force.

In 1966 his services were loaned to Hindustan Aeronautics, a firm which manufactured aircraft; but in 1963 he was called back to the air force to be Chief of Air Staff. It was the period of the second and more serious war with Pakistan. He knew that he had to neutralize the enemy air force at the outset and he sent the Canberra light bombers out to destroy their airfields. The first wave proved to be ineffective, so he at once threw in his fighter force of Mig 21s to strafe and bomb the runways. The tactic worked. Having complete command of the air, the Indian army was able to move with absolute freedom. The consequence was the liberation of Bangladesh and the breakup of Pakistan's hold on their territory in the east. This was the highest achievement of his public life.

In 1973 he returned to Indian Air Lines as chairman and managing director when it was on the verge of collapse. Within two years he had restored health and profitability, but in 1976 he fell foul of the dictatorial prime minister, Mrs Indira Gandhi. He had obtained approval for the purchase from the Airbus company of the wide body a-3000B2 aircraft. The deal was for 100 million US dollars. Since no agency was involved in marketing, substantial commissions awaited disposal; approximately 9 million dollars. Pratap knew that it was the common practice to pass on commissions to powerful politicians, and that he was expected to do this and to take his own share, which would have made him a dollar millionaire. However, he instructed Airbus not to pay the commission and to keep the money as credit for future spares. When this became known the politicians let out a squeal of rage. Mrs Gandhi summarily dismissed him.

In 1977 he found himself out of a job and seeking anything that was offered. He was working for Tata's Indian Tube Company in Calcutta when Mrs Gandhi lost the election of 1978. The new prime minister, Morarji Desai, called him back to be the first joint chairman of Indian Air Lines and Air India. When Mrs Gandhi returned to power in 1980 she once again summarily dismissed him. But this time it hardly mattered, for he was suffering from chest pains and the main concern was his survival on this earth.

Over the years I saw more of Pratap and his family than any of my friends. His father and mother came to London after the war and they met my parents. Children and even grandchildren have visited me in America. Although I knew of his difficulties with Menon and Mrs Gandhi, whenever we met he seemed to sail in from another world of first-class hotels and expense accounts. I had only the faintest idea of the roller coaster his life had been and what his integrity had cost him. He wrote to me in July 1982, to say that he was travelling to London with Hashi for an operation on his heart. On the return trip they planned to stay with us in Virginia. He died in London just before the operation was scheduled, on 13th August 1982. Almost a decade later Hashi stayed with us at our home on Hilton Head Island, and on that occasion she told us of her life with her husband, of his outstanding virtue, and the gratitude she felt at having lived with such a man. Her marriage had been what Westerners would have called an 'arranged marriage,' though actually it was a marriage of introduction, altogether a more civilized arrangement. Their friends know that no Western love affair could have produced anything more beautiful or enduring.

The book he was writing about his career in the Indian Air Force was not completed at his death. Hashi collected his notes and finished the work, which was published in 1986.[3] She has also translated the book into Bengali.

Indians are not inclined to put up bronze statues of their heroes in public places, perhaps because the British left them so many oversized Queen Victorias and overdressed viceroys. But I would like them to put up a statue to Pratap Chandra Lal somewhere in Delhi. It requires only one just man to save a city.

---

[3] Air Chief Marshal P.C. Lal, *My Years With The I.A.F.* New Delhi: Lancer International, 1986.

APPENDIX D
Joan

Joan was my companion for twenty-eight years; from Lulsgate Bottom to the Air Ministry in London; through the sunlit years in Gibraltar; to Kinloss in the north of Scotland where I commanded a wing of Avro Shackletons and American P2Vs; to Akrotiri in Cyprus, and on to Washington, DC, where I served a tour of duty in the Pentagon. Halfway through that tour I fell in love with the United States of America and asked for early retirement from the RAF. While teaching my second year at James Madison University, Joan was hospitalized with heart pains. She recovered well and was to return home. On the evening of 5th January 1970, I drove our three children up to see her. I ushered them out—to say goodbye privately and properly—and she returned my kiss, saying, "I love you," with the same passionate conviction that she had displayed three decades earlier on the moonlit lawn of the Metro Hotel in Lahore. As I was dishing up the evening meal for the children, only twenty minutes later, a telephone call informed me that she had died of a massive heart attack.

A few months later I wrote this poem. Poetry can express succinctly what it might be embarrassing to say in prose.

Running Out of Dry Goods
Slowly we're running out
Of the things Joan bought
When she was on earth
(Who now is in earth)—
The preservatives, of course, last longer,
Canned peaches and sweet cucumbers.
But I'm still surrounded
By all the things she made.

Her painting of a Halloween pumpkin
(Which she didn't think much of)
I hung up in the kitchen;
The indoor plants which trail in every corner
(Religiously watered);
The engraving of the Prodigal Son
Which she gave to me
To remind me of my father,
or of God the Father—it doesn't matter.
In the dining room is the oil sketch
Done just before I met her
By a visiting R.A. at a charity bazaar;
So like her—the big offered mouth
And classical profile.
When I first told her she was beautiful
She denied it, having been called 'Gobbie'
At her boarding school.
But she always wanted to hear it again.
"I'm not just a pretty face," she'd say.
But gradually 'her' house
Is becoming 'my' house
And I'm resenting it.
All this time I've been housekeeping
And childminding for her
Till she comes back—
Which she will, of course,
On the Last Day;
On my last day;
Dies illa—not dies irae.[4]

---

[4] *Dies irae, dies illa.* (Day of wrath, that day.)
Passiontide liturgy.

APPENDIX E
Mary

My tour in the Pentagon was for the years 1965 to 1968. It was a troubled time for the U.S.A., which included Martin Luther King's march on Selma, the protests in Washington against the Viet Nam War and race riots in Newark and Detroit. Joan and I, however, had the most wonderful time, living the social lives of diplomats from a two-bedroom flat on Columbia Pike. The bar of the British Embassy on Massachusetts Avenue supplied me with duty-free liquor, and I could do something to return the extraordinary generosity of my American colleagues. The highlight of our Washington experience was meeting Mary and Lincoln Holdzkom. Mary (born Mary Foote-Stone) was Joan's first cousin, their mothers being sisters. Her great-grandfather and grandfather were both sea captains who sailed four-masted ships on the Bristol to Calcutta run. They took their wives on board and many of their children were born at sea. Her grandfather ended his career as harbourmaster of the port of Calcutta. Her father joined the prestigious Indian Civil Service and after long service retired with his family to New Zealand. In 1943, when the Pacific war was at its height, Mary met Linc Holdzkom, a young U.S. Marine captain, who was in an elite unit commanded by Colonel James Roosevelt which specialized in attacking heavily defended island beaches. They married when he was on furlough between these death defying exploits.

In 1966, Linc had a staff job at the U.S. Marine base at Quantico, Virginia, so we were living only twenty-five miles apart. We attended each other's parties, went out on the town together, and enjoyed a honeymoon of friendship. The foursome was brutally broken by Linc's death in January 1968. He was flying with a demonstration team to San Francisco and the transport aircraft they were travelling in flew into the Sierra Nevada. There were no survivors. Two years later, almost to the day, Joan died. Mary and I were married in Toronto in November 1973. My two books of memoirs could not have been written without her support and appreciation. As a tribute to her I'd like to quote my short-est poem.

> Mary is
> A cocktail party
> To which only one guest
> Is invited.

GLOSSARY

Ayah	nursemaid
Badshah	king
Barampta	offensive sortie of Tochi Scouts
Bhang	Indian hemp or 'pot'
Charpoy	bed
Chokra	boy
Chowkidar	night watchman
Gasht	Tochi Scout patrol
Gohli	ball
Jirga	tribal gathering
Khansamah	cook
Mali	gardener
Malik	tribal leader
Mehtar	sweeper
Memsahib	married lady
Pagri	turban
Palang	bed or hammock
Punkah	fan
Sahib	gentleman
Sari	Hindu female dress
Syce	groom
Tonga	horse and carriage for up to four passengers

INDEX